FACETS OF HUMANISM

Utkal Studies in Philosophy

General Editor
P.K. Mohapatra

Editors
T. Patnaik, S.K. Mohanty
G.P. Das, S.C. Panigrahi

Volume One
Action, Freedom and Responsibility

Volume Two
God, Time and Evil

Volume Three
Studies on the Purusarthas

Volume Four
Reality and Mysticism

Volume Five
Social Justice

Volume Six
Facets of Humanism

Utkal Studies in Philosophy - VI

General Editor: P.K. Mohapatra

Facets of Humanism

Decent Books, New Delhi

in association with

Department of Special Assistance in Philosophy

Utkal University, Bhubaneswar

Published by
Decent Books
D-36/A-1, Mohan Garden
Najafgarh Road
New Delhi - 110 059

Distributed by:
D.K. Printworld (P) Ltd.
Regd. office : '*Sri Kunj*', F-52, Bali Nagar
New Delhi - 110 015
Phones : (011) 545-3975, 546-6019; *Fax* : (011) 546-5926
E-mail: dkprint@4mis.com

Printed by: DP's Impressive Impressions, New Delhi - 110 059

ISBN 81-86921-03-6

First Published in India in 1999

Preface

HUMANISM, as a philosophical world-view, had its distinctive beginning with Protagoras's declaration that man is the measure of things. But this pronouncement was as startling as it became too misleading almost immediately after it was made. The centrality of human interest and human well-being that underlie the Protagorian dictum was soon to be drowned in subjectivism and individualism. Under the tyranny of Socratic objectivism and Platonic contempt for paticulars Protagorianism was suppressed and shunned as sophistry rather than understood: humanism, in its infancy, did not get a fair deal. However, concern for man and the central significance of the human point of view could never be overlooked and hence humanistic ideals kept trickling in over the ages both in Western and Indian philosophical speculations. The Buddha's stress on the here and now, the Mīmāṁsakas' vision of *puruṣārtha* as *puruṣāya ayam*, Kant's copernican revolution and his approach to human beings as ends in themselves — all strive to make the point that man is the centre of the universe. Protogoras's dictum after all gets a resounding acceptance in the modern version of humanism in F.C.S. Schiller and even Jean Paul Sartre, with the spectre of subjectivism taken care of by transpersonal standard of objective knowledge and truth. The abstract metaphysical standard of objectivity was exposed for what it is. Be it language, morals, knowledge, truth or reality, nothing has significance (is any of these conceivable?) if it is not concerned with the human world. For nothing human can be alien to man and nothing *un*human can be fruitfully discussed. It follows, therefore, that humanism is opposed to transcendentalism and supernaturalism insofar as they are unconcerned about man and the social reality. "A mortal's god lies in helping fellow-mortals", said Pliny the Elder, and "service to man is service to God", said Gandhi. Every sphere of discourse must therefore recognise the dignity of man and the human value, take note of the person as an autonomous being endowed with free thinking and freedom of the will.

Humanism thus has to assume the most pervasive proportions. This, however, may have the danger of making it appear too simplistic and too much trivial. Indeed, one finds now a days almost everybody engaged in some sort of intellectual exercise claiming to be a humanist. Careful study of the logic of the concept with its various aspects need to be done. Essays included in this volume aim precisely at this objective. They are grouped under two parts. In part I the essays generally focus on the meaning and implications of humanism as a philosophical doctrine and the ones in part II examine the application of the concept to different spheres of life and intellectual discourse.

The editors are grateful to the scholars and philosophers for their illuminating contributions to this volume. The University Grants Commission deserve our gratitude for the grant to publish this book under the D.S.A. programme. We thank M/s Decent Books, New Delhi for associating themselves with our Department of Special Assistance in the publication of the volume.

Utkal University **P.K. Mohapatra**
8 October 1998

Contents

Part I
The Concept

Editorial Introduction

Humanism, Scientism and Religion

Sarat Chandra Panigrahi

HUMANISM is not a distinct body of doctrines, though certain seminal tenets of humanism can be reconstructed from the reflections and writings of philosophers, scientists and litterateurs at large. Humanism as an articulated mode of thinking can be traced to certain socio-politico-religious developments in the post-medieval time. It was the time when people, by and large, began to rethink and question the long-assumed beliefs and practices. Humanism came to signify the doctrines which assumed the centrality of man.

> A man becomes a humanist when he comes to see that bases of all moral thought is neither nature nor super-nature, but the specifically human.[1]

Indeed, humanism as a characteristic philosophy approach came in sharp reaction to supernaturalism and religious authoritarianism of certain theo-centric systems. Barring few, almost all the religious ways of thinking take God as the central reality and the ultimate arbiter of things and events. Explicitly in such frameworks man is construed to have a subordinate and contingent entitative status. Religious zealots in their attempt to portray the greatness of God, underplay the role of the human beings so much so that one is left with a very dismal picture of man as a mere machine. The individual is stripped of the real freedom of will because irrespective of what one wills, it is the will of God that overrides the human will and

1. R.E. Garhringer, "Liberalism and Humanism", *Ethics*, October, 1955, p. 37.

action. Man proposes and God disposes goes the saying. Man inherently lacks the capacity to subvert the will of God. He/she is simply to live the way, pre-ordained by Him. This unmistakably points to the ultimate futility of human initiative. Human reason is conceived as having a limited role. The reason is good enough to conduct the mundane transactions, but it is ultimately infructuous in comprehending the nature and ways of God. Reason is to be surrendered in favour of faith. Doctrinally humanism is the natural expression of human reason to assert itself as the supreme. It is thought that only such presupposition can explain the autonomy of the human agent and the fact of human creativity and initiative. Supplementing the views of Protagoras that "man is the measure of all things" Dakin observes,

> Man is not only the measure, but to an indefinable extent the master and the creator of reality.[2]

The period of renaissance witnessed the reign of reason which paved the way for development of science and technology. The quickening pace of scientific achievements led to the growth of scientism and the humanity stepped into the other extreme of the scale where one was led to think that reason is infallible and absolute. There is nothing which cannot be brought with in the compass of reason. The whole of nature is amenable to causal explanation. In extreme form the scientific development led to the death of the divine and the emergence of man as the master of creation. Reason is not only adequate to unveil the secrets of nature but also the nature of man himself. There is nothing in man that can elude the grasp of reason. Human behaviour is as much subject to causal explanation as the events of nature. Mind being the function of the brain, human actions become subjected to certain inexorable laws. It is the instinctive propulsions and circumstantial variables that determine how an individual is going to act in a particular existential situation. Ideally, if a man is in know of the sum-total of antecedent conditions, the behaviour-pattern of the individual can be predicted and mapped *a priori*. Seen in this perspective, the so-

---

2. A.H. Dakin, *Man is the Measure*, Princeton University Press, 1939, p. 24.

called freedom attributed to man turns out to be more apparent than real. This scientism in its extreme form leaves no room for free-will and choice. Besides, the naturalistic explanations present a myopic vision of man whose thinking and action is subject to stimulus-response dynamics. It obviously fails to take cognisance of the ethical self within by virtue of which the human beings have the sense of right and wrong, ends and means. Value awareness is undoubtedly one of the distinguishing marks of human agency. The humanistic thinkers were awakened to the urgency of protecting human identity in face of the dehumanising effects of scientism. This led to the rise of individualism, liberalism and *laissez-faire* in social, political and economic sphere respectively. Needless to say that individualism was in unfortunate fallout of the humanists' attempt to promulgate the superiority of man. By way of asserting the supremacy of the human individual, the interest of the individual was considered to be of ultimate concern. As a result individualism led to the exploitation of individuals and collective group. In the political domain liberalism was the very tone and tenor of the social institutions or corporate bodies: liberty, equality and fraternity were the catchwords and the cardinal values.

On the other hand, the principle of non-interference witnessed the phenomenon of free competition, unbridled individualism and the rise of capitalism. If individualism accounted for the reign of selfishness, intra-human conflicts, liberalism led to utter negligence of individual in favour of the so-called collective body and capitalism caused growing disparities and decadence of human values.

It is now worthwhile to see how the human thought-currents find their expression in different theoretical frameworks especially pragmatism, existentialism and dialectical materialism. For a pragmatist, human utility is the basic parameter by which the worthwhileness or viability of a thing is determined. Things and events have value insofar as they are conducive to or instrumental in promoting human interest. This tacitly points to the intrinsic worth of man. Pragmatism obviously makes a case for man as the end of all forms of socio-political engineering. Pragmatism steers clear of the extreme positions of idealism on the one hand and realism on the other.

> Humanists, at all events, will have a special motive for discarding both the old labels. For some of them hitherto had been accustomed to describe their doctrines as realistic, others as idealistic; others have varied their descriptions as the exigencies of exposition seemed to require. For them, at all events, it will be simpler to regard the doctrine we have developed as neither realistic nor idealistic but as humanistic.[3]

Existentialism is nourished by the basic distaste for essentialism which found expression in the speculative thinking of the idealists. Obsession with theoretical interests made one oblivious to the concrete problems of life. Existentialists urge to shift one's attention from theoretical speculation to pressing problems pertaining to human problem. In the existential framework man is portrayed as a willing and choosing agent inherently capable of making or unmaking his own destiny. It reposes absolute faith in human initiative and holds man responsible for all his choices and actions. The autonomy of a moral agent is obviously paramount in existential literature.

The dialectical materialism of Karl Marx had for its basis an overwhelming concern for the suffering humanity perpetrated by the capitalistic system. Marx, a great humanist, felt the compelling urge to espouse an exploitation-free stable social order where the interest of every individual is safeguarded and there is no need for anyone to thrive at the cost of others. Man is pictured as a free ratiocinating agent whose ultimate well-being consists in participating in the social process which moves from the state of anarchy to a state of order. Against this backdrop, it is imperative therefore to underline the core characteristics of humanism and examine if humanism in theory and practice is at variance with religionism on the one hand and scientism on the other.

If humanism is to be accorded the status of a distinct philosophical creed, it is bound to encapsulate a metaphysics and an ethics within its fold. Every norm or an ethical paradigm presupposes a vision of reality.

---

3. F.C.S. Schiller, *Studies in Humanism*, London, Macmillan, 1907, p. 19.

> Actually, humanism as a philosophy represents a specific a forthright view of the universe, the nature of man and treatment of the human problem.[4]

> A humanism is necessarily unitary instead of dualistic, affirming the unity of mind and body; universal instead of particular, affirming the continuity of man with the rest of life, and of life with the rest of the universe; naturalistic instead of supernaturalistic, affirming the unity of spiritual and the material. . . .[5]

Humanism is broad based on the metaphysical vision that man is the most evolved creature hitherto and rational thinking is the *sine qua non* of human thinking and action. Such a vision obviously assumes the autonomy of the moral agent, capable of second-order thinking. Unlike his co-primates man does not take things for granted but is capable of self-transcendence in subjecting what is given and what is thought to rational scrutiny. He had not only the capacity to distinguish between value and disvalue, but has the capacity to follow the good irrespective of the constraints. This precisely secures the dignity of the moral agent. Man is neither a machine nor a biological being subjected to the impersonal forces of nature but a self-asserting and self-governing rational being.

Interestingly, any attempt to get hold of the core of humanism amounts to making a case for true religion. Because religion *per se* does not mean sects or creeds that divide groups and societies, but is one which describes the way of making the righteous use of reason. In asserting the essential divinity or holiness of man, it ascribes the real dignity to man. Besides, it infuses the cardinal values of love, tolerance, fellowship, sacrifice which make man truly human. Religion *per se*, when practised in letter and spirit, is bound to work towards real equality in the social plane in fighting out the man-made differences. It holds out lofty optimism in urging

4. C. Lamont, *The Philosophy of Humanism*, London, Barrie and Rockliff, in association with Premberton Publishing Company Ltd., 1965, p. 9.

5. J. Huxley, *The Humanist Frame*, London, George Allen and Unwin, 1961, p. 14.

that man can grow into godhood or to the likeness of God. Thus a true religion is more humanistic than the so-called humanism. A humanism broad-based on religion is bound to embrace the whole cosmos within its fold.

> Do not injure another, love everyone as your own self, because the whole universe is one. In injuring another, I am injuring myself, in loving another I am loving myself.[6]

But unfortunately the so-called humanists mistake sects or divisive cults as religion and seek to defend humanism against them. In fact, the metaphysical underpinnings of both religion and humanism are one and the same.

In the same breath it can be shown that scientism and religion are not mutually antithetical. Science assumes the superiority of human intellect or reason. Scientific knowledge helps one understand 'man' better and better by exposing the artificial distinctions of caste, colour, sex and nationality eventually leading to the formation of a social order inhabited by rationally awakened individuals conscious of their duties and obligation. By trying to nourish human reason it paves the way for a dogma-free social set up. In real life-situations, human welfare is the focus of progress. If technology is not used to promote human interest, it is said to be clear instance of misuse. Hence true scientific-enterprise is at the core value-centric. Devoid of humanistic values, science results in utter disaster. Humanism provides the much needed direction for science. Humanism on the other hand should be broad-based on reason. Devoid of rational and scientific spirit, there is a risk for humanism to degenerate into individualism, thereby fermenting intra-human conflicts.

As a result humanism in its bid to promote human interest leaves humanity a divided house. Hence humanism in order to be truly humanistic must grow by drawing the best from science and religion.

---

6. Svāmī Vivekānanda, *Vedanta Philosophy*, Calcutta, 1982, p. 12.

Humanism in Indian Thought*

Ashok Vohra

LET me begin with the question 'What is humanism?' I am aware that in answer to this question one cannot expect either an analytic definition outlining someone essential or unique feature which shall be both necessary and sufficient for our using the term 'humanistic'; nor can one expect a paradigm. I neither expect analytic definition, not do I look for a paradigm, because like Wittgenstein I believe that the concept of humanism, like all other concepts, is a family resemblance concept. Indeed the term has been used in a variety of senses in different periods of history. *The Oxford Dictionary of Philosophy* (1994) tells us that humanism in the Renaissance sense "was quite consistent with religious belief, it being supposed that God had put us here precisely in order to further those things the humanists found more important. Later the term tended to become appropriated for anti-religious, social and political movements." However, it tells us that as a movement humanism is "distinctive of the Renaissance and allied to the renewed study of Greek and Roman literature: a rediscovery of the unity of human beings with nature and a renewed celebration of the pleasures of life, all supposedly lost in the medieval world". In the twentieth-century post-modernists and some feminist writers have used the term 'humanism' as a pejorative term to be applied to philosophies "that rely upon the possibility of the autonomous, self-conscious, rational, single self and that are supposedly insensitive to the inevitable fragmentary, splintered historically conditioned

---

* First published in *Philosophy and Democracy in Asia,* ed. by Philip Cam, In-Suk Cha and Mark Tamthai. Republished by permission of the author.

nature of personality and motivation". In its current usage the term connotes "any philosophy concerned to emphasise human welfare and dignity, and optimistic about the powers of unaided human understanding". According to N.K. Devaraja, "Humanism is an attitude towards and an approach to man's life and values regarded as phenomena confined to the earth." Its characteristics are "interest in man, concern for man, and faith in man's reason and conscience for discriminating perception of truth and goddness".[1]

Humanism one may conclude, is a system of views based on respect for the dignity and rights of man which values his personality, and is concerned with his welfare and all-round development. It endeavours to create favourable conditions for social life. Humanism is the opposite of fanaticism, regionism, intolerance and disrespect for the views and knowledge of others. One of the basic trends of humanism is the freedom of the individual. A humanist, therefore, is one who believes in the dignity and autonomy of man. He is averse to advocating man as dependent on any being — be it God or any other supernatural power. He regards man to be the master and the pivot around which the world revolves.

In the Indian tradition, represented by the six orthodox and the two heterodox schools of philosophy, man, his growth, development and self-realisation is a perennial theme. However, it must be noted at the outset that the concept of man in the Indian tradition is radically different from the Western concept. The scriptural literature of the West, particularly the Judaeo-Christian, tells us that the very life of man is the result of the original fall, which in turn is the result of original sin. On this view every man is considered to be a born sinner who should be ashamed of his very being, his very existence. The consequence of such a view is that a person's outlook towards his own self is full of self-condemnation and self-pity.

On the other hand in the Indian tradition men are supposed to be *amṛtasya putrāḥ*, childern of immortal bliss. According to *Śrīmad Bhāgavatam* (XI. ix. 28):

The Divine one having projected (evolved) with his own

1. N.K. Devaraja, *Humanism in Indian Thought,* Indus, 1998, p. 16.

> inherent power various forms such as trees, reptiles, birds, insects and fish was dissatisfied at heart with all these; he then projected the human form endowed with the capacity to realise *Brahman* (the universal divine self of all), and became extremely pleased.

The *Aitareya Āraṇyaka* declares that man is the abode of *Brahman*: *ayam puruṣo brahma-lokaḥ* (II.13).

The traditional Indian concept of man is quite intricate and complex. It describes it in two ways: (1) on the basis of *kośa*'s or sheaths; (2) on the basis of *śarīra*s or bodies.

According to the first description a person is constituted of five *kośa*s, sheaths one inside the other. *Taittirīya Upaniṣad*, II.2, presents each of these commencing from the second as another interior self — *anyo'ntara ātman* and adds that the succeeding one fills the preceding one — *teṣām eṣa pūrarṇaḥ*. According to *Taittirīya Upaniṣad* the outermost sheath is the *annamaya*. It is made of the intake — the food we eat, the drinks we drink, the air we inhale. This is the same as our physical body as is revealed by sense-organs. Inside this outer sheath is the *prāṇamaya*, i.e., biospherical sheath, inside which is the *manomaya*, i.e., psychical sheath. Inside the *manomaya* sheath is the *vijñānamaya*, i.e., the noospherical sheath. The fifth and the last sheath which forms the core is the *ānandamaya* sheath. There is no corresponding concept in Western thought for this. The nearer equivalent of the concept of *ānandamaya* may be the astrophysicist Fred Hoyle's notion of 'background material'.

According to second explanation a person is constituted of three bodies each inside the other. The outermost is the *sthūla śarīra*, the gross body. (It corresponds to the *annamaya kośa* in the previous description). It is the physical body of man. This material body or the physiological organism is visible to everyone and is subject to growth, ageing, death and decay. It is the subject of physiology and anatomy. It is constituted of five elements — fire, air, water, earth and space. On its decay these five elements are dissipated. Inside the *sthūla śarīra* is the *liṅga śarīra* or *sūkṣma śarīra*, i.e., the subtle body. It corresponds to the next three *kośa*s of the first scheme, namely, the *prāṇamaya*, *manomaya* and *vijñānamaya kośa*s. The subtle body is of the size of a thumb and is constituted of nineteen elements: five subtle sense-organs, five subtle organs of action, five subtle attributes (*the tanmātras*), mind, ego-sense, intellect and the self. The subtle body constitutes almost the entire content of man's personality and is with him till he attains liberation (*mokṣa* or *nirvāṇa*). It is the focal point of the Indian theory of *karma* and reincarnation. In modern times it is the subject of neurology and para-psychology. It is like the homunculus. Inside the subtle body is the *kāraṇa śarīra*. It corresponds to the *ānandamaya kośa*. There is nothing corresponding to it in Western thought. It is immortal, eternal, unchanging, spiritual, conscious and blissful:

> These three are referred to as bodies because they are the products of matter in its gross and subtle forms. They constitute the non-spiritual lustre of the truly spiritual part of man, *Ātman*.

Before undertaking a serious philosophical enquiry man takes one or the other of these *kośa*s or *śarīra*s as his true self. But philosophical enquiry reveals the not-self character of each of them; it reveals that each one of them is an object and not a subject; each of them, to use Buddha's terminology, is a *saṁghāta* or aggregate and therefore subject to change and destruction. A deeper philosophical investigation reveals the facticity of memory. The fact of memory conjoined with the underlying unity of experiences of man shows that there has to be a changeless centre in man. It is the changeless subject, or knower at the centre of the knowing process. As Śaṅkara affirms in his *Vivekacūḍāmaṇi* (121, 126):

> There is some entity, eternal by nature, the basis of the experience of egoism, the witness of the three states (of waking, dream and sleep) and distinct from the five sheaths, who knows everything that happens in the waking, dream and sleep states, who is aware of the presence or absence of the mind and its functions; and who is the basis of the notion of egoism.

This is the *ātman*, the true self of man which is also the self of the universe, i.e., *Brahman* or *puruṣa*. "The *puruṣa* alone is all the universe" —*puruṣa evedam viśvam*; "This (manifested universe) is only *Brahman*, the Immortal" — *brahmaivedam amṛtam* "This *ātman* is all this manifested universe" — *idam sarvāṇi yad ayam ātmā* proclaims *Muṇḍaka Upaniṣad*, II.1.10; II.2.11 and *Chāndogya Upaniṣad*, VII.25.2 respectively. *Bṛhadāraṇyaka Upaniṣad*, II.5.19 categorically asserts: "This *ātman* is *Brahman*." *Muṇḍaka Upaniṣad*, II, ii, 7, clarifying the nature of *ātman* or *Brahman* further says: "He is the all-knowing one, the all-seeing one, whose glory is this universe." *Chāndogya Upaniṣad* (VI.8.7-16.3) tells in powerful language that in

> this *ātman* is sustained the entire acitivity of the cosmos. It is the cosmic energy in which all the forces of nature are unified. It is the universal constant in nature controlling all its movements and processes. It is unborn and eternal. It is non-composite and indestructible. It is devoid of sorrow, without hunger and thirst.

It is pure in essence, subject neither to sin nor suffering says *Kaṭhopaniṣad* (*Vallī*, V. ii). It is infinite. It cannot be surpassed or transcended. It is absolute because it is not conditioned by space, time and causality. This *ātman* or *Brahman* is not confined only to nature outside, that is, nature spread out in space and time but is specially manifest in the depth of the being of man himself. "His presence is felt through speech and mind and thought." Such is the importance of *ātman* in Indian tradition that *Bṛhadāraṇyaka Upaniṣad* (LI.4.5) categorically asserts: "The *ātman* alone is to be seen to be heard and thought about and meditated upon."

Ātman is not different from man — each one of us. *Chāndogya Upaniṣad* declares *tattvam asi* — "That thou art". The Upaniṣads teach us, therefore, that man is not finite,

> that he is not the limited truncated thing he considers himself to be. He seems to be limited bcause he is viewed, or he views himself through the limitations of the body and the senses. In his esential nature, however, he is pure being, pure consciousness, and bliss — *sat, cit, ānanda* — and as such, he is one with all. Pure consciousness cannot be divided by the manifesting media of bodies and minds.[2]

---

2. Svāmī Ranganāthānanda, *The Message of the Upaniṣads*, Bharatiya Vidya Bhavan, 1987, p. 105.

But due to ignorance, *avidyā*, man forgets his true nature. The primary concern of the whole of Indian tradition — be it Jainism, Buddhism, Sāṁkhya-Yoga, Pūrva Mīmāṁsā or Upaniṣads, or Dvaita, Advaita, Viśiṣṭādvaita or Dvaitādvaita; be they the philosopher teachers Śaṅkara, Rāmānuja, Madhva or Nimbārka; the saint poets Kabīra, Tulsīdāsa, Guru Nānaka, Dādū Dayāla, Raidāsa, Thirrukul; or Rāmakṛṣṇa Paramahaṁsa; Svāmī Vivekānanda, Śrī Aurobindo, Ramana Maharsi and the like — is to liberate man from ignorance through educating him of his true nature. The purpose of education is to make him aware of his divine character, of the fact that he *is* verily *Brahman.* This knowledge is attained by a conscious effort to discipline the body, the sense-organs and the *manas*. It may be noted here that the Indian tradition lays a lot of emphasis on the body. It considers that "the body, verily, is the primary means to the higher life". (*śarīramādyam khalu dharmasādhanam, Kumārasaṁbhavam*, V.33). And *Mahābhārata* (XII.169.28) says:

> Immortality as well as mortality are established in the body (of everyone); by (the pursuit of) delusion, one reaches death; by (the pursuit of) truth one attains immortality.

A proper education leads man not to identify the self with the finite and perishable consituents such as body, sense-organs, *manas*, ego, etc., either individually or collectively, but to correlate himself with the infinite and the eternal. Whereas the identification with the former leads to bondage, the identification with the latter leads him to freedom and immortality.

As Śaṅkara says in his *Vivekacūḍāmaṇi*, verse 160,

> The dull witted man thinks he is only the body; the book learned man identifies himself with the mixture of body and soul. But the sage, possessed of realisation through discrimination, looks upon the eternal *ātman* as his self and thinks, 'I am *Brahman*' (the self of all).

Since *Brahman* is perfect and pure, perfection and purity are the true nature of man. This led Vivekānanda to say:

> Not to become pure, you are pure already. You are not to be

perfect, you are that already.[3]

But due to *avidyà* man has become ignorant of his own true nature. So he needs to be educated.

The aim of education, according to the Indian tradition, is to lead the individual to *vidyā*, knowledge — the knowledge which liberates him from the limitations of *avidyā; sāvidyāyāvimuktayé*. As Śrī Aurobindo pointed out:

> the seers of ancient India had, in their experiments and efforts at spiritual training and the conquest of the body, perfected a discovery which in its importance to the future of human knowledge dwarfs the divinations of Newton and Galileo, even the discovery of the inductive and experimental method in science was not more momentous.[4]

The knowledge received from the sages and seers has not to be accepted as a gospel truth. It has to be examined by each individual in the light of his own experience and on the level of the criteria of rationality accepted in his times. As Buddha syas in the *Aṅguttara Nikāya*, part three:

> This I have said to you O Kālāmās, but you may accept it, not because it is a report, not because it is a tradition, not because it is so said in the past, not because it is given from the scripture, not for the sake of discussion, not for the sake of a particular method, not for the sake of careful consideration, not for the sake of forbearing with wrong views, not because it appears to be suitable, not because your preceptor is a recluse, but if you yourselves understand that this is so meritorious and blameless, and, when accepted, is for benefit and happiness, then you may accept it.

On many other occasions too, Buddha taught the same thing to his disciples:

> As the wise test gold by burning, cutting and rubbing it (on

3. Svāmī Vivekānanda, *Complete Works*, Vol. VII, pp. 52-3.
4. Śrī Aurobindo, *The Upaniṣads*, Śrī Aurobindo Birth Centenary Library, Vol. 12, 6.

> a piece of touch stone), so are you to accept my words only after examining them and not merely out of regard for me.

Vivekānanda too, in the same vein says:

> Believe not because some old manuscripts are produced, believe not because it is your national belief, because you are made to believe it from your childhood; but reason it all out . . . then if you find that it will do good to one and all, believe it, live up to it and help others to live up to it.[5]

Each doctrine in the Indian tradition has to satisfy human reason. There is primacy of reason in the Indian tradition. Reason according to this tradition is the most precious possession of man. "Reason is supreme among man's faculties" says *Gītā*, II.42. It "helps man to cross beyond the taint of delusion and ignorance." (*Gītā*, II.52) Man has to endeavour to develop and keep it bright and pure. He has to avoid indulging in activities which weaken and destroy reason. "The *ātman* is realised by subtle seers endowed with the keenest reason", says *Kaṭha Upaniṣad*, III.12. And *Gītā* time and again says, "Through absence of reason man fails to know the immutable nature of the highest reality" (VII.24); "when man's reason is impure he fails to realise the self as it is" (XVIII.16); "It is purified reason that helps man to know right and wrong, fear and fearlessness, bondage and liberation." (XVIII.30)

But neither reason nor the mastery or complete understanding of the scriptures regarded as sufficient for *mukti*, *nirvāṇa* or self-realisation in the Indian tradition. As *Kaṭha Upaniṣad*, II.23 categorically states,

> This *ātman* cannot be attained by study of the scriptures, sharp intellect, not by much hearing.

It again says:

> not by the Veda is the *ātman* attained, nor by intellect, nor by much knowledge of books.

Bṛhadāraṇyaka Upaniṣad exhorts the seeker of true knowledge

5. Svāmī Vivekānanda, *Complete Works*, Vol. I, p. 117.

"not to seek after the knowledge of the books, for that is mere weariness of the tongue" (IV.4.21). It is quite significant that there are several passges in the Vedas and other literature of India which openly proclaim that the *ātman* cannot be attained through a mere study of them. Few scriptures in the world have the courage and boldness to say this of themselves. The Vedas could say this boldly because their search is not for a dogma or a creed but because their endeavour for the search for truth is sustained by the spirit of detachment and objectivity.

To realise the *ātman* which is one's true self, in the Indian tradition besides *śravaṇa* (hearing), *manana* (rational understanding) and *nididhyāsana* (deep meditation), one has to have its direct experience, *sākṣātkāra* or *anubhava*. This is of much greater importance than the mere study of the scriptures and philosophical systems and the knowledge gained from them. Śaṅkarācārya in his *Vivekacūḍāmaṇi* (verse 54) explicitly states:

> The true form of reality should be known through one's own *bodhacakṣu*, clear eye of understanding, and not through (the proxy of) a scholar; the true form of the (full) moon should be known by means of one's own eyes only; how can it be known by proxy?

The emphasis on direct experience is the reason why the Indian philosophers, e.g., Gautama, Kaṇāda and Kapila, develop their philosophical concepts and systems without any reference to scriptural texts.

To achieve *anubhava* or *sākṣātkāra* one has to make an effort and engage in *svādhyāya*, self-study. There are many ways in which a person can attain self-realisation. He is absolutely free to choose anyone of them and then consciously follow it. With the right effort, the goal will be reached. The purpose of the Indian scriptures is to acquaint a person with the several paths leading to *mokṣa*. But they in *no way* either guide, or direct or interfere in a person's choice. They leave the choice entirely to the individual. This is amply demonstrated by the example of *Gītā*. In *Gītā* Kṛṣṇa allows Arjuna to question him critically, shows him various paths — *Jñāna-yoga*, *Bhakti-yoga* and *Karma-yoga* — following which liberation can be achieved. He appeals to Arjuna's intelligence and heart at various levels, uplifts him to new and higher dimensions of vision and experience, but at the end of it all he tells Arjuna: *yad icchasi tad kuru*, "Now do as you wish, and decide". In his choice and effort man is not helped by any scripture. Even Buddha attained elightenment due to his own effort. It was only through his own human effort and not with the aid of some super-human or supernatural revelation or a *guru* or teacher that he achieved enlightenment. *Śrimad-Bhāgavatam* too (XI.vii.19-21) says the same thing:

> In the world men . . . uplift themselves by themselves from all sources of evil. For a human being, particularly, his *guru* or guide is verily, his own self; because he achieves his welfare through the help of direct sense experience, and through inference based on it.

Man has to give up the stagnation of sense life, leave his dogmatic slumber and make an effort to be dynamic. That is why Yama says in *Kaṭha Upaniṣad* (III.14): "*uttiṣṭhata jāgrata*— Arise, Awake!" After attaining elightenment Buddha gives a similar clarion call to his fellow beings in *Itivuttakam* II.10: "Let the awakened ones hear this (message); they who are asleep let them awake. To be awake is more beneficial than to be asleep; to the awakened, there is no fear." And his last words before passing away were: "Strive on with diligence" (*Dīgha Nikāya*, II.154). Śaṅkara says: "Arise! O creatures immersed in the sleep of beginningless ignorance: may you turn in the direction of knowledge of the self!" Vivekānanda exhorts his followers thus: "Arise, awake and stop not till the goal is reached!" The goal is liberation from *avidyā*, the root cause of the feeling of finitude in us, and attainment of real knowledge, *vidyā*, that is, realising true nature of oneself which makes him self-established, supremely tranquil, and fulfilled. This state is achieved *here* and *now* in this very life and not in a transcendental-world, or hereafter. As *Kaṭha Upaniṣad* says: "For one who realises it here (in this world) there is true life. For one who does not so realise it, great is the loss." The one who realises that the true nature of man is ever pure, ever perfect and ever illumined *ātman* attains *jīvanamukti* (liberation in life). For liberation, *mukti* or *nirvāṇa*, does not depend upon going to higher and higher spheres outside of oneself, nor on the death of the physical body (*cf. Īśa Upaniṣad*, 1.14).

In Indian tradition perfection has to be achieved by man in this very life. That is why it attaches great importance to man. Man is seen as the sole doorway to the mystery of existence. He is both a *kartā*, actor and a *sākṣī*, spectator of the drama of existence. *Aitareya Āraṇyaka* (II.3.2-3) elucidates the uniqueness of man in the following words:

> He who knows more and more clearly the self, obtains fuller being. There are plants and tress and animals, and he knows the self more and more clearly (in them). In plants and trees, verily, sap only is seen, in animals consciousness. In animals the self becomes more and more clear, because in them sap also is seen, while thought is not seen in others (in some animals). The self is more and more clear in man. For he is most endowed with intelligence, he says what he has known, he sees what he has known, he knows tomorrow, he knows the world and what is not the world. By the mortal he desires the immortal, being thus endowed. As for the others, (namely) animals, hunger and thirst comprise their power of knowledge. They say not what they have known, they see not what they have known. They know not tomorrow, they know not the world and what is not the world. They go so far. The experience ofbeings are according to the measure of their intelligence.
>
> This man is the sea (a reservoir of unsatisfied desires); he is above all the world. Whatever he reaches, he desires to be beyond it.

Vivekānanda concludes from this:

> A human being (is the) greatest being. Man is higher than all animals, than all angels; none is greater than man. Even the *devas* (gods) will have to come down again and attain to salvation through a human body. Man alone attains perfection, not even the *devas*. . .[6] (And) There is no limit to the power of the human mind.[7]

---

6. Svāmī Vivekānanda, *Complete Works*, Vol. I, p.142.
7. *Ibid.*, p. 131.

The sages in the Indian tradition take it as a realised fact, rather than a philosophical speculation, that man is essentially *nitya-śuddha-buddha-mukta-svabhāva paramātman* — the eternally pure, awakened and free self. He is neither to be identified with the body nor with the senses, including mind. Body and mind are the manifestations and instruments of his action in the spatio-temporal world. In essence he is limitless. Man alone has the capacity to realise this truth due to his unique psycho-physical system combined with the psycho-social environment created by himself in the course of his life. He alone can solve the mystery of his existence by transcending himself. Moreover, he is the only creature who has self-awareness and who is conscious of the vast energies lying dormant within him. He has the will and determination to surpass his limitations, that is why there is a constant struggle in him to get over his limitations. Through their teachings the Indian seers create an atmosphere of alertness, the mood of constant seeking, a deep passion for truth, a constant desire to forge ahead and not to take things for granted in a complacent spirit. Indian seers and sages tell him that by appropriate training of body and mind man cannot only achieve joy of health and character; excellence in beauty, culture and civilisation but also gain delights of transcendental experience, what Buddha calls *lokottara*, that which is beyond the world of the senses and the sense bound. For him the body, in fact the whole of the psycho-physical organism, becomes the finest instrument that nature has designed to help in the manifestation of true self— *brahmāvalokadhīṣaṇām* (*Bhāgavatam*, XI.ix.28).

But man, as *Kaṭha Upaniṣad* (II.6) says,

> has lost his bearings in the delusion of wealth and power, *paramādyātma vittamohena mūḍham*.

As a result he has totally submerged in nationalistic, racial, sectarian and various other forms of limiting milieus. He has to redeem himself. Indian tradition does not undermine or underplay either wealth or power or politics or society. According to it man shall have wealth; man shall have power; man shall have a healthy body and a healthy mind; man shall have social and political systems; man shall have religious sects and creeds. He can have all these, but he has to treat each one of them as means and not ends.

Man shall not be exhausted by them. He shall transcend them by a conscious effort and realise that all of them are his limited expression, whereas in reality he is limitless, infinite and eternal.

The goal of the peculiar metaphysical conception of liberation or perfection elaborated in the Indian tradition is to evolve a man"in whom there is no crookedness, no falsehood and no deception" (*Praśna Upaniṣad*, I.16). He sheds the notion of 'mine' and 'thine'. He does not say "This is my country; that is a foreigner" rather for him the whole world becomes his family, *vasudhaiva kuṭumbakam*. His word and deed are not vitiated by the sentiments of triviality, of limitation, of finitude, of exclusiveness, of separateness.

In conclusion, one can say that the Indian tradition is humanistic in that it believes in human freedom, reason, responsibility, and autonomy and summons man to a constant struggle to gain the highest, and to achieve the eternal and the permanent. But at the same time it must be noted that the Indian notion of humanism is different from the Western notion. In the West man is seen as a dominator of external nature, as a creator of values in society. For example, according to the Promethean spirit in Greek thought, human spirit has the power to overcome external obstacles and establish man's supremacy over the forces of nature and, if necessary, over other human beings as well. One of the defects of this way of thinking is that it does not carry all humanity together. Another is that it leads to egoism in man.

The Indian tradition chastens and overcomes the egoism in man by making him a part of nature, a part of the cosmos. He is one with others. No one is either superior or inferior. He is one with all and all are one with him. I am *Brahman*, and so are you. So all men are equal. So, there is no one to be conquered. When man achieves supreme self-transcendence, he finds that there is nobody to dominate. He discovers a universal man integrated within and without, pulsating in the heart of man and nature. He becomes one with the cosmos and the cosmos merges into him. This insight and integration of man with his external world gives him courage and capacity to see life steadily and see it as a whole.

The Human Point of View

Bijoy H. Boruah

HUMANISM must be human-ism in some form or other — a theoretical outlook on the significance and centrality of the human individual in the scheme of things. The problem therefore is how this significance and centrality attached to the individual is to be interpreted and its theoretical underpinnings articulated. Something about the very idea of an individual's being a *human person* in relation to other such individuals as well as other animals and the natural environment has to account for that significance and centrality.

An individual's being a member of the class of *homo sapiens* is what makes one a human being. But what goes into the making of a human *person* is the kind of *consciousness* that is able to generate certain attitudes — attitudes to oneself, other human persons, and the world as a whole. Central to these attitudes is what might be described as the attitude of agency and freedom — in short, free agency. Indeed, there is something depersonalising about someone who lacks this attitude altogether — one who always has the experience of lacking the sense of agency.

It is not so much the idea of agency but the idea of *freedom* that is relevant to the elucidation of what I would like to call 'the human point of view'. I would also add that it is the human point of view that accounts for the distinctiveness of the human person. Furthermore, humanism, as a theory about the existential role and significance of the human person, is to be expounded by reference to the so-called human point of view. This point of view is unique because of the uniqueness of the freedom that I consider central to a human person.

Attributeless Personal Essence

Inter-personal relation, whether of communication or of other modes of social exchange, is the phenomenon that needs to be explored here. Whether an individual is entering into a truly human relationship with another is determined by whether the individual adopts the human point of view in the act of establishing that relationship. And the adoption of the human point of view is an attitudinal matter, it is a matter of internalising an attitude essentially characterised by freedom. Indeed, it is an attitude of freedom. But what is the peculiarity of this notion of freedom?

Crudely speaking, it is freedom of the mind. And it is the peculiar potentiality of human consciousness to be capable of yielding such inner freedom. Here I venture to say that this freedom consists in our very special ability to think of one another in what might be described as the *attributeless* or *non-predicative* mode. When a human person is thought of as a person in the non-predicative, attributeless mode, the person is not regarded as a creature of some kind, characterised by this or that property. Rather, the person is regarded just as *someone*, as a unique but bare particular. He or she is *meant* as the person *per se* — that is, just himself or herself. As a *self*, in virtue of which someone is himself or herself, the person is essentially attributeless.[1]

Being a person is, both minimally and maximally, being able to be *oneself*. It is this key idea of 'oneself' that underpins pronominal expressions such as 'I', 'he', 'she', 'you' and 'me'. As personal pronouns, these expressions have a peculiar designative function. Each uniquely designates a bare personal particular, a pure personal essence as it were. And the indexicality of the expressions is evidently indicative of the 'purity' (bareness) of their designative role. That role is to pick out the person, not as the possessor of certain attributes, but as an attribute-independently conceivable personal essence — as a *self* in short. The notion of the self as a unique bare particular is aptly captured in the metaphysical idea

1. I owe the idea of the attributeless mode of thinking to Ramchandra Gandhi. See his *The Availability of Religious Ideas*, London: Macmillan, 1976, especially chapter 2.

of the *soul*. But while the idea of the soul is submerged in the ineffable mystery of speculative metaphysics, it finds a metaphysically neutral non-speculative characterisation in its elucidation as the pure or attributeless personal essence of a human individual. This elucidation is also metaphysically innocent in that there is no implication of the materiality or immateriality of the human self conceived of as a bare particular. The only implication is that a human individual would not be a person if it could not be a self, and that being 'oneself' is independent of the attributes of personal contigencies.

Non-attributive Attitude and First-order Significance

Given this idea of 'oneself' as attributeless personal essence, it invites the question of the *accessibility* of a person in his or her pure personal essence to another fellow person in a situation of personal encounter. Any personal encounter is not *ipso facto* the realisation of a relation between two human individuals at the level of non-attributive or non-predicative purity of personal regard. Whether such a 'pure' relation is realised depends upon the adoption of the non-attributive mode of regard by one individual towards another. There is thus such a thing as the non-attributive attitude, by virtue of which one frees oneself from the clutch of the predicative or attributive mode of personal relation. The character of human relations is, more often than not, shaped by, and framed within, the attributive-predicative mode of regard towards one another. The person appears, or stands out, as an individual of this or that type, with specific features perceived to constitute his or her personhood. His or her personhood is reductively identified with their possessing those features, and terms of negotiation based on those features are settled. Human commerce is then turned into a calculated play of utilitarian culture controlled by instrumental rationality.

I now want to maintain that the human point of view consists, in essence, in the adoption of the non-attributive mode of thinking when one human individual views another in a context of personal or social relation. This, however, does not mean that attributes of personal contingency are immaterial or irrelevant to the human point of view. Rather, what is contrary to that point of view is the attitude of relating to a person *solely* in terms of the properties that he or she has, howsoever desirable or otherwise these properties may be. There is something *counter-human* in one's enduring and persistent tendency to recognise another as a human person of significance or insignificance exclusively from the standpoint of the importance or unimportance of the attributes belonging to that person.

What is counter-human about the exclusively attributive attitude — or, perhaps more accurately put, the attributively signifying attitude — is its betrayal of the truth that a human individual is, *qua* a person as such, a centre of attributeless significance. Pure personal essence is just another name for this centre of attributeless significance. I consider this to be a fundamental truth about the very idea of personhood. Any attributively accorded significance of a person is a second-order significance of the person who has first-order significance by virtue of being a person as such.

Thus, to think that human significance consists merely in the acquisition of attributes generative of second-order significance is to fail to realise the fundamental sense of (first-order) human significance. The notion of first-order human significance is foundational to the very idea of human personhood. As such, this notion is expressive of what we might take to be the *basic humanity* of all human members. The human point of view is the viewpoint of recognising first-order significance and, hence, basic humanity.

Intrinsicality

It might be alleged, against my position outlined above, that to accord first-order significance to human persons is not really to adopt a non-attributive attitude. Rather, it amounts to adopting an attributively signifying attitude because persons are being viewed as having the attribute of first-order significance. This would mean that, far from being centres of attributeless personal essence, each person is accorded the common attribute of being a (significant) person as such, which in turn would imply that, the so-called human point of view is no less an attributive attitude than that of according second-order significance.

This allegation would miss the point of the talk of different orders of human significance and the special meaning of first-order significance. Spelt out, first-order significance just means that a person is attribute-independently significant. Therefore, to give *this* notion of significance the status of an attribute would be tantamount to talking about the attribute of attributelessness. But this is circumlocutionary and at most rhetorical. At worst, this is like saying that something has the value of having no value at all.

More importantly, first-order, attributeless significance is *intrinsic* to personhood, and this significance is duly appreciated only when one relates oneself to another person from the non-attributive stance. In contrast, second-order significance is *extrinsic* in that it accrues to a person's life in the contingent development of that life. It accrues to a person as he or she begins to 'create' a certain kind of life. This significance is contingently acquired as and when a person paves a path in the life-world.

Essence Precedes Existence

If the human point of view as elucidated above is to determine the recognition of basic humanity, which in turn is supposed to ground humanism, then there emerges a certain view of humanism that sets itself against one well-known form of humanism — namely, the existentialist humanism of Sartre. Existentialism as humanism rests on the key idea that 'existence precedes essence' — that is, there is no essence to a human person independently of what the person does by way of creating a life of its own. There is no first-order significance inherent in personhood because there is no personal essence that is logically or temporally anterior to the person's actual existential engagement. To be is to choose to be something and thereby to acquire for oneself attributes of significance.

If existentialist humanism is anti-essentialist, the form of humanism that might emerge from the human point of view defined in terms of the non-attributive attitude is going to be essentialist. But it would be essentialist in a non-substantial sense. For it implies no more than the existence of a centre of attributeless significance in the form of pure personal essence. There is no implication of a soul-substance as the source of that essence.

Perhaps it is this form of non-substantive essentialism that underlies Wittgenstein's remark: "My attitude towards him is an attitude towards a soul. I am not of the *opinion* that he has a soul."[2]

I am inclined to defend such an essentialist approach because it seems to capture the idea of basic humanity as well as human dignity in a uniquely suitable way. At the core of the principle of basic humanity and human dignity lies the idea of human equality. It is quite obvious that humans are not equal at the level of attributes of second-order significance. But the ethics of human dignity requires that human equality be secured in a manner that also articulates the principle of basic humanity. I therefore think that we must have recourse to the attributeless level of first-order significance as the only level of securing equality. It thus seems to be the best way of laying the ethical foundation of a plausible form of humanism.

Deep Ecology

So far I have tried to sketch a theory of the human point of view within the orbit of inter-human personal relationship. The question that urgently awaits consideration at this point is whether this theory has anything interesting to say about the adoption of the human point of view towards non-human animals and the natural environment. The real question, in short, is whether the proposed theory is resourceful and comprehensive enough to provide a basis for animal and environmental ethics.

Again, I am inclined to answer in the affirmative. If I, as a human person, am able to relate to another fellow human person from the non-attributive viewpoint, there is no reason why I cannot take the same stance towards non-human animals and the natural environment. Adopting this attitude towards animals and the environment would mean taking them for what they are, independently of their utilitarian or instrumental significance. And the non-instrumental attitude makes available to us the idea of a world of animals and natural environment as endowed with

---

2. Ludwig Wittgenstein, *Philosophical Investigations*, tr. by G.E.M. Anscombe, Oxford: Blackwell, 1958, Part II, section iv.

intrinsic significance.

Of course, in claiming this I am not indulging in personification. I do not want to hazard the risk of saying that, like human persons, there is pure animal essence and pure natural environmental essence. The claim rather is to suggest that the human point of view, shaped by the non-attributive and non-instrumental attitude, especially conduces to our ethically relevant identification with the animal and natural world.

The argument that sustains this suggestion is rather plain. If a person is genuinely able to purge his or her mind of the attributively signifying attitude towards other fellow persons, then the person is to that extent able to transcend anthropogenic limitations of a crucial sort. It is a human limitation not to be easily able to see someone in terms beyond second-order significance. Hence, being able to rise to the level of first-order, attributeless significance is an example of ascending to a qualitatively superior level of humanity.

Now it seems intuitively clear that a person with this sort of qualitative attitudinal ascent would surely rise above exclusivist anthropocentric attitudes. Indeed, there is something highly counterintuitive about the idea of a person who respects a fellow person with non-attributive attitudinal purity *only because* the latter happens to be a member of the same human species to which the former belongs. This would amount to human species chauvinism and hence it cannot dovetail with qualitative attitudinal purification.

Exclusivist anthropocentricity is the central impediment to human identification with the non-human world of animals and natural environment. Thus, if the truly human point of view transcends anthropocentricity, then the possibility of adjusting animals and the natural world within our ethical space is always open to us.

Epilogue: Cosmocentrically Human

In visualising the possibility of rising above anthropocentric species-chauvinism through the capacity of cultivating the non-attributive attitude, I have presumed human consciousness to have a unique depth and freedom. Being able to see another person in his or her attributeless essence is also expressive of lifting oneself to the level of attributeless purity. Indeed, the latter, self-directed attitudinal ascent is a precondition for other-directed non-attributive mode of personal regard. Pure personal essence has to be realised within oneself in order that others are seen as instantiating that essence.

I now want to say that the unique depth and freedom of human consciousness has the remarkable efficacy to let human beings excel themselves. For pure personal essence is an attitudinal perspective that 'abstracts' the human person out of anthropocentric species-specificity. That (non-attributive) perspective finds its new anchorage in cosmocentricity. Perhaps this is a human privilege available only to human consciousness. If freedom from species-specificity is indeed a human privilege, then *that* is the centrality of humans in the cosmic order. That is my theory of humanism.

Human Beings as Autonomous Persons
On Legitimising the Humanistic World-view

Ramesh Chandra Pradhan

THIS paper is concerned with the question of the legitimisation of humanism as a philosophical world-view. Humanism is a metaphysical standpoint which is based on the idea that human beings constitute an autonomous domain of reality. This view has been accepted by philosophers who question the legitimacy of the world-views that deny the autonomy of the human beings. Humanism is thus in direct confrontation with the religious authoritarianism of the past ages. It also no less conflicts with the so-called scientific hegemonism of the present age. It is therefore imperative that we search for the legitimisation of the humanistic world-view itself.

In this paper my effort is to draw an outline of the metaphysics of man that is the foundation of the doctrine of humanism. I will argue that it is the question of the autonomy of the human person that is the central question of humanism and not its socio-political implications. I do not take into account humanism as a socio-political theory or creed in this essay. The more fundamental question in this respect is the question of the human reality itself *vis-a-vis* the non-human world.

The Metaphysics of Man and the Limits of Anthropocentrism

Humanism as a philosophical doctrine has developed out of a concern for man, that is, out of the realisation that human beings occupy a central place in the universe. That man is at the centre of the universe has slowly dawned upon the philosophers after Kant's

Copernican Revolution[1] in philosophy. It is not that in the earlier ages man's importance was not realised, but with Kant philosophy recognised the central place of human beings in the metaphysical scheme of the universe. Man thus is made the Archimedian point of the new universe.

But with the rise of man into the centre of the world came the demand that man is no more a slave of Nature and that she is not a mere accidental product of the Darwinian natural selection. The Darwinian naturalisation of the human species was questioned by philosophers as it led to a loss of the image of man as a creative being in the world with superior intelligence. The evolutionary picture of the universe in the post-Darwinian period consists in depicting the human beings as the masters of Nature rather than slaves of it. This view is in conformity with the view that human beings are autonomous beings with a capacity to rise above the natural order of things.[2]

The philosophy of man that gives rise to humanism as a new metaphysical world-view puts emphasis on the following points:

(a) that human beings are radically different from the non-human Nature,

(b) that human beings are self-conscious and self-governed beings making a community of human individuals according to the rational principles.

The first point is the very crux of humanism in that it recognises the fact that human beings constitute a distinguishable domain that is different from the domain of the material bodies and the animals and plants. Though it was realised that the human species is a natural species likes plants and animals, it was increasingly felt that the human species has a distinct existence.[3] The second point brings out more clearly that human beings are not merely intelligent

1. See Kant, *Critique of Pure Reason*, tr. by N.K. Smith, Macmillan, London and New York, 1929.
2. *Ibid*. Also see L.W. Beck, *A Commentary on Kant's Critique of Practical Reason*, Chicago University Press, Chicago, 1960.
3. See J. Agassi, *Towards a Rational Philosophical Anthropology*, Martinus Nijhoff, The Hague, 1977.

creatures but are also self-conscious individuals that can command dignity and self-respect. This brought to view the fact that human beings are also persons who are endowed with self-consciousness. Locke's[4] famous distinction between persons and human beings made this point more accentuated. The result was the clear recognition of persons as a distinct metaphysical category not on a par with the natural beings such as animals and plants. Persons are human beings considered as the autonomous individuals in a community of self-conscious persons.

The idea that human beings constitute a distinct metaphysical category facilitates the new awareness that human beings are not mere natural objects of anthropological research and that they are the subject-matter of metaphysics in the sense that they could very well be studied for the sake of self-understanding. This idea of understanding man as a self or person gives rise to the idea that man ceases to be a natural being at certain point of her evolution and becomes a new individual with the capacity of self-understanding. Thus the anthropological view of man and her life is sought to be delimited by a metaphysical view of the meaning of the human persons. The Darwinian categories have utterly failed to understand the nature of man. Therefore there has been an effort to project a rational philosophical anthropology[5] to undertake the investigation into the nature of man as a rational being. The rationality of man consists in her capacity to think of herself as a meaning-pursuing being.

The Birth of a Person

The birth of a person is the greatest event in the evolutionary history of man. This has occurred not because of a natural selection or mutation of the human genes, but because of the new developments in the history of the self-awareness of man. Self-awareness is the key to the conception of a person. Persons are the human beings who are self-concious. Therefore there arises the

---

4. See Locke, *An Essay Concerning Human Understanding*, Fontana/Collins, 1964, chapter XXVI.
5. Cf. Agassi, *Towards a Rational Philosophical Anthropology*.

conflict between the naturalistic-scientific understanding of man and the philosophical understanding. The scientific understanding is confined to thinking of man as a natural being or a physical object or at best a biological species. This view does not take account of the fact that human beings are more than a biological species. The philosophical view of man brings in the fact that human beings have the capacity to think, to remember, to judge and so on. This crucial fact about man that she is a thinking being was emphasised by Descartes and since then has never been given us as a cardinal belief about man. The idea of a person therefore has much to do with the Cartesian notion that man is a thinking being.

The notion of a thinking self or soul is the foundational idea in the philosophy of persons for the following reasons:

(a) Persons cannot be conceived except as the human beings who have the capacity to think, that is, except as those who have the propensity to have ideas and judgements. This is the fact the Cartesians have emphasised in their conception of a person.

(b) Persons are the beings who have the capacity to remember a large part of their lives and thus have the idea of their self-identity and self-knowledge.[6] This is how the idea of self-image of man has become a defining property of a person.

Thus the nature of a person has been associated with such ideas as soul, self-consciousness, memory, etc. The problem of how persons are possible is therefore the main metaphysical question in this respect.

There are basically two metaphysical conditions of there being persons. They are, (1) that the persons are self-individuating and they are capable of realising their autonomy as distinct individuals, and (2) that they are self-constituting and meaning-giving human beings. While the first condition makes the idea of autonomy of the individuals the crucial concept, the second makes the notion of the

---

6. See Shoemaker, *Self-knowledge and Self-identity*, Coronell University Press, Ithaca, N.Y., 1963, for the role of memory in the conception of person and personal identity.

constitution of meaning as the central activity of a person. Meaning in this sense has to do with the entire gamut of our life and actions. The persons are involved in the activity of constituting meaning while being engaged in the activities of life. Meanings and actions together constitute the life of a person.[7]

The birth of a person thus is the birth of meaning in life which has its origin in the capacity to realise one's autonomy. Persons are endowed with the capacity to think of themselves as the autonomous beings; therefore they have the capacity to realise their dignity and uniqueness. The person makes the idea of herself internal to her self-consciousness and thus arrives at the idea of the dignity of self. The self is the ultimate origin of the value I as a person pursue. Besides, I realise that my personality depends on nothing other than myself to have self-respect. I have the dignity and the self-respect as a person and not as belonging to this society or that. My social position is derivative and conditional, whereas my being a person is metaphysical and unconditional. This unconditionality is the true source of the meaning of my life.

Meaning of life and value go together. Life is valuable in a metaphysical sense. Therefore everything associated with life is valuable provided it does not contradict the value of life itself. If the material enrichment of life contradicts the original value of life, then the former must be taken as a disvalue, otherwise not. Thus we have to limit the concept of value within the circumference of our life as a person or self, and not as a social creature. If we extend the circumference too wide, then the very centrality of personhood will be diluted to the extent of disappearance of value altogether. As long as the person enjoys her autonomy as a unique individual in the unconditional sense, there is value and meaning of life. Freedom of the will and the other features of the personhood follow as a corollary from the unconditioned notion of a person.

From the above, of course, it does not follow that the human existence in the physical world is forgotten altogether. That is, it is not the case that human beings cease to be what we ordinarily call

---

7. See Charles Taylor, *Human Agency and Language*, Cambridge University Press, Cambridge, 1985.

the natural beings. Their natural life is not denied; rather their non-natural life is emphasised. The non-natural life includes the facts of meaning and value such that a person as a value-pursuing individual is brought into focus. the question is not whether human beings are embodied beings or not, but whether we can talk about the meaning of life without any reference to their physical existence. Physical embodiment is the lowest denominator of the personhood of man because the body does not constitute the person at all. Only thinking beings are persons and therefore the non-thinking beings cannot become persons. Otherwise, trees, pots and pans could also become persons. The latter can become persons provided they can think, talk and do many things like us.[8] But such a possibility is ruled out precisely because the trees and pots do not have the capacity to think.

Human Beings vs Machines

Human beings are type-distinct from the animals and plants. This is so because as a species the humans have a distinct identity. For good or bad they have certain capacities which the non-human species lack. For example, we cannot conceive of the animals speaking or the trees philosophising. As Wittgenstein says: "If a lion could talk, we could not understand him."[9] This is not because lions have a superior language which we cannot understand but becuse lions have no language at all. We understand the lions as they are, but we cannot understand the speaking lions. The fictions about the plants and animals talking are just fictions which increase our curiosity about them, but they do not reveal themselves as real speakers at all.

The philosophical debate as to whether the humans and the non-humans could be put under the category of the machines has relevance in this context because the humanists in all ages have protested against the view that the human beings can be treated as

---

8. Cf. Anthony Quinton, "The Soul", *The Journal of Philosophy*, 59 (1962), pp. 393-409.
9. Ludwig Wittgenstein, *Philosophical Investigations*, tr. by G.E.M. Anscombe, Blackwell, Oxford, 1953, II, xi, p. 223.

no more than machines. The view that human beings are sophisticated machines with linguistic as well as intellectual abilities has been there since the time of Hobbes and other materialists who deny that man has a soul or a mind distinct from the body. The contemporary philosophers of mind who have tended towards materialism[10] have not rejected the view that man is a kind of machine and that the so-called mind is nothing other than the brain which can be mechanically simulated. The brain functions like a machine according to the machine-functionalists.[11] Thus there is a growing opinion that the human mind could be machanically represented in an artificial system of mechanical functions. This view thus reduces the functions of the mind to a set of mechanical functions represented in a machine like a sophisticated computer.

Now we can see that if the humans are ultimately machines and the human mind can be artificially recreated in a machine, then there is no justification for humanism as a philosophical theory. In fact, humanism has to surrender its claim that there is autonomy of the human species. Mechanism rather than humanism will be the order of the day because we all will be united under the category of Man-as-machine. Such a scenario is not only degrading but also disgusting. First of all, it is a philosophically pernicious doctrine that human beings are glorified machines. Secondly, it is factually false that human beings behave like machines. The philosophical truth about man is that she has creativity[12] and that human intelligence is natural which can be simulated to some extent but cannot be reproduced mechanically. Thus we must admit the fact that the possibility of man being a machine is logically ruled out as

---

10. See John Searle, *The Rediscovery of the Mind*, The MIT Press, Cambridge, Mass., 1994, for a critique of the materialist philosophy of mind.
11. See Hilary Putnam, *Mind, Language and Reality, Philosophical Papers* Vol. 3, Cambridge University Press, Cambridge, 1975. Essays 18-20 for a discourse on the functionalist and computational view of mind.
12. See Searle, *The Rediscovery of the Mind*, chapters 4-6 and 9 for a discussion on the nature of the subjectivity of human consciousness.

it directly contradicts the type-independence of the human species. The scientific truth about man is that human beings do not behave as machines at all. Human behaviour is notoriously unpredictable while the behaviour of a machine is controlled and predictable. We are therefore bound to attribute free will to human beings but not to the machines. Thus there is a moral and metaphysical gap between the human beings and the machines.

Machines cannot be self-conscious entities even if their artificial intelligence is hundred times more than that of the humans. The supercomputer is still a computer that depends on human agency; it cannot be a self-evolving system aiming at its own perfection. Humans do revolt against their present state and evolve into a better state of existence. Thus the free creativity which humans possess is lacking in the robots and computers. Thus there cannot be a state of affairs in which the machines can recreate themselves into meaning-seeking persons. Machines under no circumstances can attain the personhood which is unique only to human beings.

Humanity as a Metaphysical Presupposition

The crux of the matter is that humanity is a basic datum for the humans. The essence of the human beings is their humanity which can be made into an abstract principle. The principle of humanity as Kant conceives of it is such that it is the foundation of all morals and actions. Kant says:

> The ground of this principle is: rational nature exists as an end in itself. Man necessarily thinks of his own existence in this way: thus far it is subjective principle of human actions.[13]

Thus the human nature is taken as an end in itself and is treated with respect for the reason that it is the basis of our moral and social life. The principle of humanity thus makes it possible how human beings can understand themselves as well as others.

---

13. Quoted in Christine M. Korsgaard, "Kant's Formula of Humanity", in *Immanuel Kant: Critical Assessments*, Vol. III, ed. by Ruth F. Chadwick, Routledge, London and New York, 1992, p. 170.

The Kantian view of humanity and humanism paves the way for the theory that it is the human beings who have to be taken as ends and not as means to any other end. This means that the human beings must be treated as the autonomous agents who have dignity and self-respect. In nature man is found not as a means to any higher goal, but as the goal of the biological evolution. Human beings represent the highest development of the biological world. In society also man is not the means of a higher social goal. Rather she is the goal of the society itself as she is the fountain of the very social structure which is built around her. Human welfare is the goal of the social organisations. Therefore it is legitimate to say that all political and social theorisations must recognise the metaphysical reality of humanity.

Humanism as the term itself suggests makes the principle of humanity its basic presupposition. According to this principle, the human beings are the ends of our moral and social endeavours and hence we must recognise the human beings as autonomous agents. The idea of end is very crucial in this context because human beings are quite likely to be treated as means of the society or the state or other individuals. In the history of human civilisation human beings have been subjected to inhuman treatment because they have been used as the means to certain ends. Economic and social exploitation has been endemic in human history because man's essential humanity has been overlooked and her autonomy has been compromised.

Humanism as a metaphysical world-view therefore takes for its foundation the essential humanity of the human beings. It presupposes that human beings are metaphysically autonomous and that they are moral agents who not only aim at higher and better life but also lead a life of nobility and happiness. This would not be possible if the basic dignity of man is not realised. Therefore, it is right to say that

> Humanism asserts human dignity and the freedom of the human spirit; it is a kindly philosophy.[14]

---

14. David Ehrenfeld, *The Arrogance of Humanism*, Oxford University Press, Oxford, 1978, p. viii.

The dignity of man is the *sine qua non* of any conception of society because a society is supposed to preserve it. Morality itself is grounded in the dignity of man as it proposes ways and means to preserve and enhance it. Thus the very idea of humanity is the idea of human dignity as an autonomous individual.

Freedom of the individual is the unique feature of the humanistic society that is based on the principle of humanity. Freedom here stands for the unhindered growth of the individual as a human agent. His basic potentiality is allowed to flower into manhood without hindrance from outside. Thus the human spirit enjoys freedom that accrues to it as a part of its autonomy. Humanists have celebrated human freedom along with the human dignity.

The First Person: The Possibility of Spiritual Humanism

It is the first-person that provides the clue to the understanding of the human self . Man viewed as a subject is the first person that is an 'I'. The 'I' brings out the sense of the human subjectivity. There is a fundamental distinction between man viewed as a subject and she being viewed as an object. The latter is given to a third-person view of the human beings. In the third person account of man, we have necessarily to refer to human beings as some sort of objects. The external features of the human being are projected in the third-person point of view.

Humanism protests against the view that man is an object and that his existence can be given only a third-person account. Science in general, physical sciences in particular, takes man as an object in the sense that she leads a natural life like any other animal and lives in the spatio-temporal world. Science therefore fails to account for the subjectivity of man which is the basic fact about her from the first-person point of view.[15] The subjectivity disappears altogether from the scientific point of view as it fails to explain how the inner being of man is possible at all. The subjective dimension of man reveals her inner life, the unique experiences that characterise her

15. Cf. Thomas Nagel, *The View from Nowhere*, Oxford University Press, Oxford, 1986, chapter IV.

self and so on. Thus the experiences which are uniquely individuated in the self of a person are sought to be reduced by the scientists in their zeal to naturalise the human beings.

There are limits to the naturalisation of man since at certain point the whole reduction process gets deflated and the subjectivity of man emerges as of central importance. It becomes impossible to reduce the self further though certain features of man are definitely reducible such as her experiences which are triggered by the brain. The brain being a central mechanism in the human body it is possible that some of our experiences are directly linked with the brain and therefore are reducible to the brain states. But the subject of these experiences, that is, the 'I' or the self itself cannot be so reduced. Even the brain requires as a person or subject to which it can belong as the brain by itself is not the subject.

Subjecthood is unique to man as an experience and also as an agent. The subject is not a mere logical necessity for experience to be possible, but also a metaphysical necessity. The subject must exist so that the experiences are individuated. That is why there is so much metaphysical weight attached to the concept of 'I' or the self. In the absence of a person, there is not only no action but also no experience. This fact leads to the view that the 'I' is the transcendental subject of human language, actions and experiences. The transcendental subject is the very ground of language and experiences. In this sense the self has a metaphysical locus which is outside the limits of the factual world.[16] The self thus is demonstrated to be not an object but a metaphysical presupposition of the world.

Humanism fully recognises the possibility that man is not a mere object in the world and that it is the subject which is the foundation of morality and religion. Thus it recognises that man is a spiritual entity. By being a spirit, the self does not lose its subjectivity but gets its subjecthood accentuated. The spiritual subject is the culminating point of the process of the evolution of the human consciousness. The more we realise that the spiritual

16. Ludwig Wittgenstein, *Tracatus Logico-Philosophicus*, Routledge and Kegan Paul, London, 1961, 5.632.

subject is the metaphysical reality, the more we realise that man is to be treated as an autonomous being. The autonomy of the human agency follows from the fact that the human self is a metaphysical subject. The metaphysical subject can very well be taken as the spiritual subject.

Now the question is: Is not spiritual humanism the authentic humanism that can correctly interpret and understand human beings? From the present perspective, the answer is affirmative in the sense that human beings can be properly understood only as the spiritual beings who are conscious of themselves as autonomous. It is not metaphysically necessary to believe that human beings are disembodied beings to be spiritual beings. All that is required is that the human beings realise themselves to be different from the physical objects. The fact that the human existence is the matter of philosophical understanding rather than of scientific investigation does suggest that man belongs to the category of self, the person and the spiritual being. Once this is realised it is easy to find that there cannot be anything called scientific humanism.

Scientific Humanism: The End of the Road

The very idea of scientifc humanism suffers from the fact that it contradicts the real spirit of humanism. Scientific study of man misinterprets the human reality itself. It objectifies the human existence and leaves out of account the meaning of human existence. That is why science conflicts with humanism. The following passage from Julian Huxley shows the basic commitments of scientific humanism:

> I use the word Humanist to mean someone who believes that man is just as much a natural phenomenon as an animal or a plant, that his body, his mind, and his soul were not supernaturally created but are all products of evolution, and that he is not under the control or guidance of any supernatural Being or beings, but has to rely on himself and his own powers.[17]

17. Margaret Knight (ed.), *Humanist Anthology: From Confucious to Russell*, Barri and Rockliff, 1961, pp. 159-60.

If this projection of scientific humanism is carried forward, it can lead to a metaphysical disaster as it cannot explain how man's autonomy is possible except for the fact that she is not created by God. It can reduce man to the level of animals but cannot show how the human agency in morality is to be accounted for. The death of supernaturalism that it asks for is counter productive because it denies the very autonomy of the self. It denies the uniqueness of human existence. Thus scientific humanism reaches the dead-end of the road to the discovery of the self.

The arrogance of scientific humanism as shown by David Ehrenfeld issues from the fact that it has

> supreme faith in human reason — its ability to confront and solve many problems that humans face, its ability to rearrange both the world of Nature and the affairs of men and women so that human life will prosper.[18]

This faith, however, has been misplaced because mankind has ended up in the destruction rather than the prosperity of human life. The world is yet to be redeemed by the scientific humanists. There is much to be desired about the spiritual progress of man. The promise of the future therefore lies in the emergence and the reassertion of spiritual humanism. Einstein presents the following model of a spiritual man which is worth considering:

> A person who is religiously enlightened appears to be one who has, to the best of his ability, liberated himself from the fetters of his selfish desires and is preoccupied with thoughts, feelings and aspirations to which he clings because of their super-personal value.[19]

Such a man represents the true spirit of spiritualism as she embodies in herself the essence of the spirit of humanity and is also elevated to the level of super-personal existence. Thus spiritual humanism does assert that man has a transpersonal existence.

---

18. David Ehrenfeld, *The Arrogance of Humanism*, p. 5.
19. Margaret Knight (ed.), *Humanist Anthology*, p. 152.

Humanism
Philosophy of the Post-Modern Man

Ganesh Prasad Das

HUMANISM is said to have a long historical background as the meaning of the word 'humanist' has varied from age to age to cover a range of attitude and opinion from Democritus to Erasmus in Europe and from the Upaniṣads to Nilakantha Das in India. Some persons think that it is a rational intellectual attitude which is common to all the humanists. But it is not merely that because that can go with narrow interests and social unconcern. Two things are pointed out to be common to the humanistic thinking. Terence puts the first one thus: *Homo sum: humani nihil a me alienum puto* ('I am a man: nothing human do I count alien'). Pliny, the Elder puts the second one thus: *Deus est mortali isvare mortalem* ('A mortal's god lies in helping his fellow-mortals'). These two propositions involve certain important implications like, (i) man is not merely a spirit, (ii) man is not merely a body, (iii) man is not a doll in the hands of Nature/God/Fate and (iv) man is not a digital assemblage of 'I' and 'O'. In other words, the conception of man due to Spiritualism, Materialism, Fatalism, Scientism are thrown overboard as infertile.

Humanism is interested in the human potential and human welfare. The humanist is concerned more with changing the world than with describing it. According to H.J. Eysenck, the above-stated aspiration needs to be read along with the following statement of J.B. Watson regarding the aspirations of the science of psychology.

> Psychology as the behaviourist views it is a purely objective experimental branch of natural science. Its theoretical goal

is the prediction and control of behaviour.[1]

The humanist does not admit the religious mode of life as the right method of change and evolution of society as the worldly change is thought to be due to some other worldly thrust and human aspirations are thought to be in need of divine sanction. Yet it would not be wholly correct to call the humanist an atheist as this sounds too dogmatically certain, nor an agnostic as that would be too negative an epithet, nor even a secularist as he is, by and large, regarded to be as that would have unnecessarily too much anti-clerical fervour. To call him a free thinker would be too dated at the fag-end of the twentieth century when our speech and behaviour in what might be called a too permissive society as everybody would vouchsafe are but free and to call him a rationalist would be to talk in an excessively cerebral tone. The humanist is different from the rationalist as well as from the philosophical materialist insofar as the former aspires to influence the future in some way and the latter do not. Although his point of view is different from that of the religious thinker insofar as the latter seeks, but the former does not, to explain the natural phenomena is terms of the supernatural, both are given to faith of same kind. The religious man has faith in a deity whereas the humanist has faith in humanity. The faith in humanity is not metaphysical as the faith in a deity is, but the former is as much beyond the ken of knowledge as the latter is. The belief of humanism is reflected in the tenet laid down in the Humanist Alternative, i.e., "that human problems must be faced in terms of man's intellectual and moral resources without involving supernatural authority". It is contended that in both of its negative as well as positive aspects, humanism has to lean heavily on psychological investigations.

In its negative aspect, the aim of humanism consists in the destruction of superstition and religious belief, religious belief itself being identified as superstition. Eysenck says "that the identification of 'superstition' with religious belief is itself a superstition". His assessment is based upon the result of an experiment carried out by

1. H.J. Eysenck, "Humanism and the Future", in A.J. Ayer (ed.), *The Humanist Outlook*, London, Pemberton in association with Barrie & Rockliff, p. 265.

R.H. Thoulless in America three decades back. (I do not know if any such has been conducted here in India). He seeks to illustrate that certain liberal superstitions are there alongside of the conservative superstitions. If the latter are due to religionism, then the former are due to scientism.

In its positive aspect, the humanist desires to change the world. But in which direction is the change to proceed and by which method is it to be produced? To answer these two points psychological investigations too is regarded as indispensable because both are vitiated by traditional superstitions. Discovery of the psychological laws with regard to them would lead to their eradication. But the problem is that the psychological laws are only generalisations out of observed cases and so hold good for some of the people for some of the time, not for all of the people for all of the time. There are individual differences between people which are too deep-seated to be altered.

> People are fundamentally, constitutionally, congenitally different in the most profound way from each other; no general rule or law can cover all these different needs, desires, motivation.[2]

The view that people are fundamentally different from one another is not derived from the Leibnitzean thesis that the angles of vision of no two monads are identical. This is an *a priori* statement based upon the principle of philosophical logic, identity of the indiscernible. The view is advanced on the basis of empirical investigation into the mental make-up of people. Study of random samples would not, therefore, be sufficient. Instead, observational and experimental study of individual men would have to be conducted meticulously and generalisations have to be made carefully. Such generalisations, howsoever careful and meticulous these might be, cannot be free from preconceived ideas, especially when two contending generalisations are there. I am not going to go further into the problem of pure empiricality of scientific generalisations. I am rather seeking to point out that such experiments which are bound

---

2. H. J. Eysenck, *op. cit.*, p. 269.

to be quite frequent as the present state of invasion of the premises of political people by the media people with audio and video recorders in hand shows how human beings turn into 'guinea pigs'. This is an abrogation of democratic values and might be called an antinomy of democratic form of organisation. The avowed aim of the Democratic set-up to make men free from all fetters. But his freedom is curtailed by subjecting him to all sorts of scientific experiments against his will, experiments with regard to his education, avocation, habitation and all that made by governmental authority. Things are nationalised, denationalised and renationalised. There is I.A. and B.A. courses, then Pre-University, Pre-professional and B.A., then I.A. and B.A., then +2 and +3 and then one knows not what. Like this and like that. The point I want to bring home is that experiment carries the implication of control. It is pertinent to note here that Vinoba Bhave argued 'freedom from government' as the ideal of his Sarvodaya movement. Śrī Aurobindo is reported to have said,

> the Western system grew out of the mind. They are led by reason and want to make everything cut and dried without any chance of freedom and variation. If it is democracy then democracy only. No room for anything else. They cannot be plastic.[3]

Humanism, as a point of view, was proclaimed by a galaxy of thirty-three intellectuals hailing from across section of the Western society sixty-five years back in the form of a manifesto which appeared in *The New Humanist*, May/June 1933. It was laid down as a new philosophy, not as a new creed and was said to be about matters of final concern developed out of the materials of the modern world. The creeds and religious belief coming down from the tradition could not be fit and adequate to take stock of the fast changing scenario arising out of world-wide interaction as well as exchange of knowledge, economics and goods. All these necessitated interreligious dialogues and understanding and radical changes in religious beliefs rather than small amendments therein. Religion and spirituality was not wholly decried. Religion was recognised as

3. *Evening Talks*, p. 564.

a means for realising the highest value of life and spiritual values were sought to be inculcated as the spirit comes at the apex in order of existence. The original version of humanism, then, is that of religious Humanism having fifteen affirmations which can be summed up as follows:

1. The universe is self-existing, not created.
2. Man is a part of nature and a result of evolution.
3. Human life is organic, not a juxtaposition of mind and body.
4. The religious culture and civilisation of man is a natural product of his interaction with the environment.
5. There is no supernatural or cosmic generation or sanction of human values.
6. The varieties of 'new thought' like Theism, deism and modernism are outdated.
7. All these actions, purposes and experiences, labour, art, science, philosophy, love, friendship, recreation, etc., that are humanly significant and intelligently satisfying come under the purview of religion. There is no distinction between the sacred and the secular. (This implies that secularism is subsumed under Humanism).
8. The ultimate end of human life is complete realisation of human personality. Its development and fulfilment lie here and now.
9. There would be religious emotion instead of worship and prayer as it would make personal life better and produce co-operative effort for social well-being.
10. There is no essential way for expression of religious emotions.
11. There is no place for sentimental, unreal hopes and wishful thinking.
12. Creative achievements add satisfaction to the life of man. So religious humanism encourages that.

13. All associations and institutions exist for the fulfilment of human life.

14. The goal is to construct a free and universal society in which people voluntarily and intelligently cooperate for the common good. It is a shared life in a shared world.

15. It is life affirming, not life denying and it is satisfaction of all life, not some.

The statement of Humanist Manifesto-I was considered as too optimistic in view of the march of events during the four decades since its proclamation. The hazards faced by humanity during these years include Nazi brutality, suppression of human rights by totalitarian regimes, evils wrought by science by unleashing wars in the name of peace, establishment of police states in democratic set-up and abuse of power by military, political and industrial elite. Traditional theism does not help matters. God who listens to and grants prayers of men loves and cares for them and faith in Salvationism as ultimate value are unproved and outmoded ones. They envisaged the advent of the twenty-first century in 1973 and the need of other modes of faith in view of and in commensurate with ever advancing knowledge for survival and progress of the *homo sapiens*. The proclamation of Humanist Manifesto-II, then signed by 117 individuals appeared in *The Humanist*, September/ October 1973. It came with the hope that science and technology would open the door for 'an abundant and meaningful life' and that the next century (which is now exactly one thousand twenty days ahead) 'can be and should be the humanistic century'. The modified and mitigated version of spiritualistic humanism is naturalistic humanism which seeks to "fuse reason with compassion in order to build constructive social and moral values". It has different forms like scientific humanism, ethical humanism, democratic humanism, religious humanism and Marxist humanism. It is important to note that the concept of humanism ceases to be a structural concept implying that it connotes certain essential features. It is now a functional concept insofar as anybody who advocates free thought, atheism, agnosticism, skepticism, deism, rationalism, ethical culture or liberal religion advocates humanism.

The humanist does not intend to reinterpret traditional religion because any hangover of the old is likely to perpetrate old dependancies and escapism. What is in need is radically new human purposes and goals. The goal is the survival and fulfilment of the human race. The purpose is to eradicate all the obstacles like wars, calamities of nature, diseases, divisive forces and create conditions for having the best of man's natural freedom. Belief in the existence of a supernatural is either meaningless or irrelevant to this. The humanist is an atheist in this sense as he begins with humanity, not God, nature, not deity. Hence Wittgenstein's contention that the totality of facts is God can be a maxim for the humanist.[4] Views that merely reject theism are not equivalent to humanism. It is rather

> an ethical process through which we can make, above and beyond the divisive particulars, heroic personalities, dogmatic creeds, and ritual customs of past religious or their mere negation.[5]

The humanist seeks to create a new syndrome of values which furthers social construction or rather social reconstruction. It is a fusion of head and heart, of reason with compassion. Reason and intelligence are regarded as the self-sufficient instruments with the human species. Reason needs to be tempered with humility and balanced with compassion and empathy. The humanist aspires to answer all questions and solve all problems concerning genuine human situations, but he does not have any dogmatic claim about them. Ethics is situational and autonomous; it does not look forward to any supernatural sanction or authentication, either theological or even ideological. Ethics stems from human needs and interests. So it is but evident that moral values derive their source from human experience. Plato's identification of God with the highest idea, that is, Good and Gandhi's identification of God with Truth can, in this sense, be regarded as humanistic.

A common objection against humanism is that it is unable to provide an ethical system and in effect, lives parasitically on the

---

4. *Note Books*, 1.18.16.
5. *Humanist Manifesto II*, 1973.

ethical capital of one or other of the great religion. Let me digress a little to show that this objection is not unfounded notwithstanding the claims of its advocates. Śrī Aurobindo thinks that,

> religion is integrally one with his total endeavour for the highest fulfilment of his life, his supreme value.[6]

He makes an important distinction between 'true religion' and 'religionism':

> True religion is spiritual religion, that which seeks to live in the spirit, in what is beyond the intellect, beyond the aesthetic and ethical and practical being of man, and to inform and govern these members of our being by the higher light and law of the spirit. Religionism on the contrary entrenches itself in some narrow pietistic exaltation of the lower members or lays exclusive stress on intellectual dogmas, form and ceremonies, on some fixed and rigid moral code, on some socio-political or religio-social system.[7]

It can be discerned that if Śrī Aurobindo's contentions are accepted, humanism registers its difference from religionism as well as from religion. Humanism, according to its proponents is rational and intellectual, but does neither go beyond it, not ossify into rationalism and intellectualism. When, therefore, Śrī Aurobindo asserts that religion is essentially spiritual and that it is human and natural too, his conception of humanism must be different from its post-modern proclaimants. Actually what is human, according to Śrī Aurobindo, is not the Western conception of religion, but the Indian conception of *dharma*. *Dharma* is defined that by which one attains to perfection of sublimity and of supreme Good. (*yatobhyudayaniḥśreyasasiddhiḥ sa dharmaḥ*). Man without *dharma* is not a man at all, but merely an animal, as this constitutes the distinctive characteristic of man (*dharmo hi tesām adhiko viśeṣaḥ*).

---

6. H. Maheswari's words in "Religion in the Light of Sri Aurobindo", *Sri Aurobindo's Action*, March, 1998, p. 10.
7. *The Human Cycle*, Cent. Edn., pp. 166-7.

The Humanist Manifesto II proclaims that in the best sense of 'religion', "it may inspire dedication to the highest ethical ideals". A.J. Ayer has perhaps the liberal humanist outlook when he says, "You need not come back to the old forms but you retain the spirit which might create its own new forms." His conception of the humanist outlook is that it "is not so much adherence to a given set of doctrines as having 'similar moral interests', and 'common intellectual approach'."[8] If this is appreciated properly, Humanism can very well be called a religion.[9]

The individual person is precious and dignified as our above exposition of humanism shows. Whichever religious or ideological or moral codes denigrates the individual, suppresses his freedom, dulls his intellect, dehumanises his personality is liable to be rejected. Rationality and freedom are, accordingly, the major themes of humanism.

Man's capacity to form the world, to vary it, and to better it presupposes that man is free. If God speaks in the words of Pico,

> I have placed you at the centre of the world so that from that point you might see better what is in the world. I have made you neither heavenly nor earthly, neither mortal nor immortal, so that, like a free and sovereign artificer, you might mould and fashion yourself into that form you yourself shall have chosen.[10]

People are more important than rules, regulations and prescriptions according to the humanist. But who the people are whom we meet, says Flew. But there is distinction between people and people. It is said sarcastically that some are more equal than others. (In my trade, I have heard it from friends that some are born professors and some are professors by courtesy.) We know very well to what extent this is true. But the question is, "Does the humanist treat people

---

8. Editorial Introduction to *The Humanist Outlook*.
9. A.J. Bahm's proposal, *Humanist Manifesto III*.
10. "Oration on the Dignity of Man", quoted by Nicola Abbagnano in his article on "Humanism", *Encyclopaedia of Philosophy*, Vol. IV, p. 70.

differentially?" I am sure that the humanist would resist attempts to mete out diferential treatments to people whose natural rights are the same as well as attempts to make and remake rules with interests of a chosen group of people in view. There must not be any discrimination on the basis of race, religion, sex, age and ethnos. There must be equality of opportunities and recognition of merit and talent of all. Ayer talks about the great majority of people getting the benefit of good life in the society:

> It is morally instrument upon humanity to do everything in their power to bring about the material and social conditions in which the great majesty of people will have a fair opportunity of finding satisfaction in their lives. . . .[11]

In one of my articles, I have objected to All India Radio's motto *bahujana hitāya, bahujana sukhāya* (for the beneficence of a great majority of people, for the happiness of a great majority of people). It happens, I hope, to be the Buddhistic 'ideal' leading towards pragmatism. My contention is that it cannot be an ideal proper. The ideal would be *sarvajana hitāya, sarvajana sukhāya* (for the beneficence of all people, for the happiness of all people). This is the ideal of the Advaita Vedāntin.[12] I am given to know that sometime after the publication of my article, the Brahmapur Municipality has adopted this as their motto, '*sarvajana hitāya, sarvajana sukhāya*'.

While translating the ideal into practice, one has to measure the benefit and happiness in terms of the 'common good' and the method of the same ascertaining would be socio- and psycho-metrical. That is known as the democratisation of economy. (We have witnessed recently the film awards 'in the democratic way'). The requirements of the human beings in the society as well as the results of some social planning are assessed scientifically, but such scientific explanation do not seek to take away the freedom of man.

The human being by virtue of his natural endowments does not just ditto the goals or values set in some Saṁhitā or code because

---

11. *Encyclopaedia of Philosophy.*
12. *Vide*, my paper, "What is Humanism?", *Proceedings of the Eighth Session of All Orissa Philosophy Association*, pp. 38-45.

that might have been composed in a context which is drastically different from the present one. The humanist objects, as we have noted previously, absolute viewpoints like capitalism or communism. I would like to include democracy too as being such a viewpoint. Human beings need creative values to live by. They would find expression through economic and political institutions and goals. Fundamental scientific research and technology are regarded as the vital key to human progress and development. But any trammelling of human freedom and rights is repudiated. The rights to birth control, abortion, divorce, euthanasia, suicide are upheld. Undesired use of science and technology such as cloning, production of all sorts of war-heads are decried.

The proclamation of Humanist Manifesto II said that the earlier Manifesto was too optimistic. But this itself does not appear to be less so when we look at its blue-print for the future. It visualises the building of an integrated International Community (what is otherwise called 'global village') where there must be full co-operation in culture, science, arts and technology across ideological borders. Each man must become a citizen of the world community in ideal and practice as well, because each man's failure is in some way linked to the future of all.

The humanist cultivates the pious hope that each man *eo ipso* would develop social consciousness so much to that there would not be any necessity of the state to step in to promote what are his own interests and goals. This is like the ideal of communism, viz., the withering away of the state, or the ideal of Vinoba, viz., freedom-from-government as already discussed.

I would like to conclude the paper with two or three more observations. The first is about the freedom of man. I have said that this is one of the major themes of humanism. But as we all know, freedom, in the proper sense of the term, is a far cry in this highly complex society in which the government of the day controls every aspect of our lives with the help of high technological devises. Russell argues forcefully that very few countries of the world have as yet (this is as true today as it was seventy-five years back when he talked about "Free Thought and Official Propaganda") the most elementary kind of freedom, the freedom of thought.[13] There are certain as well as subtle and elusive kinds of control on this.[14] This is so in spite of the fact that, as Ayer believes, the average man is more humane, more pacific and more concerned with social justice than he was a century back.[15]

This leads me to the second observation. I am inclined to believe with Russell that the modern world seems to be moving towards a social order imposed by force representing the will of the powerful rather than the hope of the common men. The powerful is made so by the endowments of nature, or by brain or by brawn or any combination of them. We have, therefore, said before that reason must be tempered with humility and balanced with compassion and empathy. According to Russell the philosophies that have been inspired by the scientific technique are power philosophies. They tend to regard everything non-human as mere raw material. Ends are no longer considered sacrosanct. The skilfulness of the process is alone valued. I repeat it very often that at present, there are no leaders, there are only managers in different fields. This is a form of madness, Russell says.[16] Humanism which is a brand of power philosophy is, for Russell, a brute fact, not an idea, notwithstanding the high sounding proclamations of its advocates.

Lastly, what we need is not so much the advocating humanist, but the practising humanist. Humanism is not maintained in thought alone, nor said in words alone, nor shown in action alone. It is propounded in thought, word and action — all three in perfect unison. Humanism is a value, an arch-value, for, speaking pleonastically, all the human beings. Let humanism begin from our home and then get spread to our work-place, society, state, country and to the entire globe like a drop of ink spreading gradually in a bowl of water.

---

13. Voltaire tells Rousseau, "I do not agree with a word you say, but I will fight to the death for right to say it."
14. Bertrand Russell, *Sceptical Essays*, Unwin Books, London, 1960, p. 102.
15. *The Humanist Outlook*, p. 8.
16. *History of Western Philosophy*, London, Routledge, 1996, p. 482.

Beyond Humanism

Aditya Kumar Mohanty

THE paper is an humble exercise to expound the logic of humanism and examine if humanism could be an answer to the problems and challenges in the contemporary social scenario and eventually to fortify the contention that humanism though essential, is not enough. In course of the paper, we shall address ourselves to certain central questions and dwell on the seminal issues pertaining to humanism both as an ideal and ideology and conclude with the observation that humanism, in order to be truly humanistic has got to embrace the non-human existents within its fold. Thus, a plea for Neo-humanism as the panacea for the ills looming large in the contemporary social scenario.

The Concept and the Cult

In the generic sense of the term 'humanism' is grounded in the very tone and texture of human thinking. Human thinking is predominantly anthropocentric. That explains why the man's reflections about nature, society and about himself bear unmistakable stamp of individual or social psyche. Humanism as a creed or a pattern of thinking has grown out of man's concern about himself *vis-a-vis* non-human existents. It has led them to protect and promote the interest of human species, most often, at the cost of the non-human creatures. Humanism as an articulated system of thought is of contemporary interest and is motivated by the revolt against the supposed religious authoritarianism on the one hand and Scientism on the other. It is nothing but a conscious self-assertion of man against the onslaughts of Materialism and religious autocracy. The discussions and the debate, by and large, hinge upon autonomy of human existence. On the one hand, scientism treats human being as an evolute along with other evolutes in nature, making him amenable to the laws of nature. Even the mental phenomena are sought to be explained in terms of stimulus-response mechanism of brain. Mind is nothing but the function of the brain, an epi-phenomenon. Thus, the *person* is identified with the biological being. On the other hand, certain truncated forms of religious doctrines view the *person* as essentially a spiritual being. They decry body and mind as veritable obstacles on the path of spiritual unfoldment. The thesis of providential decree is interpreted to mean that a person is a tiny cog in the cosmic wheel. Individual is a mere puppet, set to dance to the will of the Divine. In either case the autonomy of the individual becomes a necessary causality. On the one hand, the role of human reason is subject to inviolable laws of nature and on the other, it functions at the behest of the Divine. Against the backdrop of scientific determinism and divine pre-ordination the humanists claim of autonomy or freedom becomes more significant.

Salient Features of Humanism

Humanism as a system of thought and a pattern of living, presupposes the supremacy of human existence and the primacy of human goals and values. It is a fact that human beings occupy the highest rung in the ladder of evolutionary hierarchy. The role of the human species has proved to be greatly consequential not only for man or human society, but also for the environment around. In the bid to secure autonomy of the individual there have been attempts to spell out the distinctive characteristics of human species. Needless to say that the capacity for rational-thinking and freedom are central to the understanding of a human-person. Needless to state that *rationality* and *freedom* refer to the static and the dynamic aspects of the action-phenomena. Rational cogitation helps one determine the propriety and impropriety of the means and ends whereas *freedom* implies the act of pursuing a means or end, certified by rationality. The thesis of humanism boils down to the contention that man has the ability to think and act despite the limiting laws of nature and the determining laws of the providence. A *Person*, *per se*, has the inherent ability to choose a course of action deemed as rationally tenable and thereby, can carve out one's own destiny. Thus, human species unlike other, enjoy the dignity of being the free rational agents who pilot the destiny of their own lives and that of the corporate body as well. Seen in this perspective, *rational thinking* and *freedom* appear to be constitutive of the concept of *Person*. On account of being free, rational agents, human-beings play overriding role against the backdrop of natural laws and supernatural enactments. In what follows, we shall argue that the foregoing conception of man is myopic as it fails to state what is characteristically native to the humans.

The Concept of Person

A closer reflection on the notion of Rationality discloses that both Freedom and Rationality are value-concepts. Freedom has two-fold connotation, i.e., *freedom from* and *freedom to*. Negatively, it means absence of constraints or handicaps that limit the freedom of the individual and in the positive sense, it means the ability to pursue a course of action thought as rationally proper. Freedom therefore, means neither caprice nor license. Give the plurality of alternatives, one is free to choose either the proper or the improper but when one opts for the improper, one is not said to be free. For example, an action motivated by the baser urge is not taken as a free-action for one acts here under the propulsion of instincts. A doctor is free to kill or to heal. But the latter is not taken as paradigm instance of action, for the simple reason that a free-action must have as its goal, a righteous end. This takes us to the modalities of determining the propriety or impropriety of means and ends. It is here that the notion of *rationality* comes to our rescue. It is worth indicating here that Rationality, *per se*, is a mere capacity. Given the alternatives, one can have competing or overriding reasons for pursuing any one of the alternatives. A devil can quote scriptures. In other words, *rationality* can be tailor-made to justify an action which is otherwise considered to be evil. If a person is in penury he may have reasons to suffer rather than taking recourse to robbing the rich who owe their riches to foul means but another person in the same situation, may come out with competing reasons to rob the rich. So in the event of conflict in the alternative modes of rationalisation one is at a loss to find, if *rationality* does really take one to any definite end. It is rather the case that *rationality* is always at the service of one's convictions or framework. The way one reasons, discloses who the one is or the framework or the value-patterns that one subscribes to. Thus, *reason* only helps one to walk on the path pre-chartered by the implicit ends or goals. However, dexterously one may reason, it is decried as mere sophistry or humbug, if it is not directed to an end which is morally tenable. This enables us to get at the very core or essence of being a person. Rationality, worth its name, must be value-centric and goal-specific. Thus, normative-awareness, i.e., the ability to reckon a value and distinguish it from dis-value can be seen to be the *sine qua non* of human awareness. This has led thinkers to equate *rational-will* with the *good-will* or *moral-will*. By virtue of this native endowment every human being is said to possess his/her intrinsic worth, in respect of which everyone is equal to every other and deserves to be treated as an end. Hence, the Kantian wisdom that we are all members in the kingdom of ends.

Human personality is a trio in one, i.e., that is body-mind-spirit complex. When we address an individual we are addressing the three different selves, i.e., the desiring or the appetitive or the ratiocinating-self (mind) and the spirit or the normative self which sets the goal before the appetitive or the rational-self. In respect of the appetitive-self each man is unique and different from the rest whereas in respect of the rational-self there is consensus but it is provisional and relative. The fact that a group of persons reason in a particular way and thereby, arrive at a rational consensus, simply points to their unity in respect of their normative-self. It is worthwhile to point out that the so-called normative self is nothing but the pure self expressed in the agential mode (*space-time-person coordinate*).

Search for Essence

Humanism is the result of the dogged search on the part of the humans to find unity beneath the diversities. It is indeed the fact that no two individuals, groups, communities or races are identical. Besides the nature-made differences, there are differences fostered by the vested interests. Humanism rests on the fundamental vision that the perceived differences are peripheral and do not have any bearing on our being or essence, in respect of which we are all human beings. '*Human society is one and indivisible*', is orchestrated slogan of the humanists. The social reformers seek to provide a common forum for the humans, at large, urging that human beings, irrespective of the perceived or conceived differences, are identical in respect of their primal motivations, emotions, rationalisation and basic aspirations. On the other hand, a religious prophet reminds that a person is neither the body nor the mind but the *Self*. We are all the children of immortality (*amṛtasya putraḥ*). The fatherhood of God and brotherhood of man provide strong motivations to transcend the parochial or divisive tendencies, otherwise exploited by the vested interests to their convenience. Metaphysically, *humanism* is grounded on the vision of underlying unity and sociologically, it encourages the ethics of holistic living or world fraternity. A humanist, therefore, fights a pause less battle against the fissiparous creeds and cults that artificial barriers between man and man, causing alienation of man from their fellowmen.

Plea for Neo-Humanism

It is a fact of history that all religious thinkers of past were humanists at the core but the converse is not the case. For example, Darwin is said to have dispensed with the thesis of divine origin of the creation in showing that human species as much as the non-humans are subject to the inexorable laws of natural selection, survival of the fittest, etc. Marx, the great humanist, conceives of man as an economic being, actuated by considerations of bread and butter. Needless to say that there are three great thinkers who were responsible for the dehumanisation of human race. They are Darwin, Freud and Marx. When Darwin conceives man as one among the other evolutes of nature and Marx fails to take cognisance of finer psychic or spiritual nuances by conceiving man as an economic being, Freud gives no less bleak portrayal of man by tracing the genesis of all motivations and aspirations to the *Libido*. This has the unmistakable lesson that *humanism*, in order to the truly humanistic must be broad-based on the totalistic vision of human nature. Unless backed by a perennial source of human inspiration, *humanism* degenerates into crude Individualism and a set of dead habits and ends up in a fiasco, as a stray stream gets eaten up by the hot sand of the dreary desert. In other words, *humanism* in order to be a living force and offer a common platform for the people to congregate in order to care and share the weal and woe of one another, must be sustained by the feeling of unity in the very depth of our being.

Even conceding that *humanism* becomes the living ideal of the day, dissolving the contradictions and differences, bringing home the message of love, tolerance and amity, it cannot perhaps provide the ever longed relief to the ailing humanity. The humanity, today is caught up in a strange paradox when the unthought of boons of Science have proved to veritable banes. We are sitting on the precipice of ruin. Unless under guard, the creator man, may fall a sure victim to his creation. We have had surfeit of scientific and technological advancement as it were, as we are yet to learn to live with them. Science which is avowedly used to serve the cause of man is intrinsically value-neutral. It is a mere power; rich in mechanisms but poor in purposes. Without a well defined goal Humanity seems to lack a sense of direction. Time and space having been conquered, we virtually live in a global cottage where the fate of one is integrally bound up with that of the every other. At the same time we have to take cognisance of the brute fact that the humanity is an utterly divided house with the individuals and groups viewing with one another in the name of language, caste, colour, creed, nationality and what not, with the divisive sentiments (geo-sentiments, socio-sentiments and even humano-sentiments) fissiparous ideologies holding us at ransom. The saga of human development is vocal about man's exclusive obsession with his own interest with total disregard of the interest of non-human existents. The wanton destruction of the flora and fauna in the name of development, the pollution of earth, water and air caused by extensive industrialisation, depletion of the ozone layer, warming of the planet, only go to show how human species in their bid to safeguard and promote their own interest, have grown oblivious to the interest of non-human existents and the natural environment. The pursuit of selfish interest has only led them to take recourse to ways that are self-defeating and suicidal. The increasing ecological imbalance, unless put under check, is sure to render the planet unfit for human habitation. The whole gamut of social engineering and developmental programmes are humano-centric but eventually, prove to be prejudical to human interest. This precisely, is the irony of *development*. It points to the exigency of redefining man's relation with the rest of the creation and evolving an appropriate strategy of living. Hence, the existential need to look beyond Humanism.

Humanism, has all through perpetuated the inter-creature conflicts. The sense of superiority complex has led man to treat others as a mere means. Neo-humanism seeks to obviate the inherent pitfalls of humanism in pointing out the fact of cosmic interrelatedness. The universe is like a symphony. We are but individual notes in the cosmic orchestra. A thing or being, however tiny or insignificant it might otherwise appear to be, it does contribute to the richness of the melody. The manifold particulars are nothing but varied expressions of the Cosmic. Hence, everything is noble, nothing is ignoble. No creation is redundant. Everything has its existential value because by its very existence, it does contribute to the harmony of the whole, of which we, the human beings, are integral parts. Human beings do not have right to deprive others of their right to existence simply because they cease to have any immediate utility value. For that, Humanity has paid a very dear price for its inability to realise the fact that we all live the life of interdependence. The moon in the sky stimulates the growth of tiny plants on the ocean floor. How remotely they are situated but none the less, how intimate is their relationship! Hence, the Neo-humanist urges that the quest for unity which led man to discover a common bond among all humans should be extended to non-human creation, in order to see if there is some underlying essence which can bind the whole creation by the bond of cosmic fellowship. The insular vision can be sublimated and the sway of the divisive ideas and sentiments can be overcome through cultivation of the psycho-spiritual practices which result in steady expansion of the human psyche, culminating in the realisation of the cosmic unity. It has indeed, been a belated realisation on our part that, *if we are to live we must let others live*. Human beings, on account of being more evolved and articulate, carry the onerous obligation to protect and promote the interest of the less evolved ones. Such a holistic vision and conviction can only pave the way for *Cosmic fraternity*.

Humanism and the Concept of Person

Rajshri K. Jobanputra

Objective

'HUMANISM' as generally comprehended, suggests to be a perspective having a set of presuppositions that considers the human race as bearing a special position among the rest of things in the world. To state it explicitly, it upholds the most essential aspects of man that incorporates the human values, his goals, his ideal and his self-esteem. The humanist, thus focuses not only the uniquely human aspects of people but also the important aspects. The word 'humanism' came into general use only in the nineteenth century, however the humanistic mode of thinking had widened its tradition with the advent of eighteenth-century thinkers like Voltatire, Bentham, Hume, Kant and others. They did not always agree with one another, nevertheless these thinkers formed a family united in support of such values as freedom, equality, tolerance, secularism, etc. They also encouraged individual creativity, moral sense and responsibility and believed in the possibility of progress and the possibility of perfection of human nature.

The modern humanists on the other hand attribute crucial importance to education, conceiving of it as an all round development of personality and individual talents. They advocate freedom of thought and opinion, the use of intelligence and pragmatic research in science and technology, and social and political systems. Believing that it is possible to live confidently without resorting to metaphysics or religion and that all opinions are open to revision and correction. The modern thinkers today see human flourishing as dependent on open communication, discussion, criticism and unforced consensus.

This transition of values seems to have been affected by number of reasons like the industrial revolution, the rise in urban population, etc., but one of the major reasons that has been instrumental in changing the humanistic perspective is the increasing progress in the field of science and technology, an era in which human beings are conceived in petridishes and test-tubes.

The point however remains simple and straightforward that though there may be numerous ways in which the conception of human beings be manipulated, the basic human nature remains untouched, one which neither the scientists nor the philosophers can alter even by an iota. The technological advances at the most, can be said to provide us with solutions for infertility with the help of artificial insemination or *in-vitro* fertilisation. But these technologies have failed to give us 'new species of human race' (for the present the ethical issues involved in the practice of such artificial methods of reproduction have been deliberately ignored). In other words, intervention of technologies in the area of reproduction can change the physical or the genetic constitution, but it cannot alter the metaphysical nature of human beings. Technological advances today take pride in exhibiting its victory in manipulating the genetic constitution of the human, however barley successful in modifying the basic skills and abilities which the yet to be born, may inherit. It is, however, beyond the reach of any kind of technology that science has given us so far, which can modify his essential nature of being a *rational* being.

The main objective of the paper is to highlight and uphold the basic humanistic belief and doctrine that the human race indeed occupies a special place in this universe due to its nature, a nature so mysterious and elusive, that has kept thinkers and philosophers on their toes. A large part of this essay will be directed in knowing what makes the nature of man so mysterious or elusive. Being a student of philosophy, any attempt to analyse this question will be philosophical in nature. First we shall survey the basic and generally accepted views on the nature of man and then arrive at the common and fundamental nature of man. Note that my elucidation of the concept of person is essentially an attempt to know man's nature through his attributes and properties which he uniquely possess. The essay, however, will not be merely the listing of these properties, but an attempt in which the answers will be sought to the question: why these properties are specifically the attributes of man? Why the possession of these attributes forces us to refrain from treating him on par with other beings? Thus the attempt is two-fold:

1. To show what are the unique properties which can be predicated of the human beings alone, and
2. What makes these properties selectively unique suggesting the impossibility of predicating them to non-human beings?

The remaining part of the essay will be a conclusion that will follow from the answers to the above questions. In all, my basic objective is to sytematically attempt to show, by way of demarcating the characteristic properties of man, the reasons behind the claim that the attributes predicated to the humans are indeed unique and un-characteristic of other beings, that these attributes are *specie-specific*, i.e., characteristic of a specific class of specie. These predicates, in line with Ryle, if attributed to a specie of a different kind, will lead to a 'category mistake'. Thus, in saying that these attributes are specie-specific, it should be noted that the differences among the attributes predicated is one of *kind* and not of *degree*. Simple illustrations will show that the above claim does not go unwarranted.

Introduction

The nature of man has never been a mystery for the philosopher, a fact evident from what once Aristotle stated, 'that man is a rational animal'. A similar idea echoed in the works of the modern American philosopher Ayn Rand who extends the Aristotelian and upholds the thesis that reason is man's only tool of survival. Thus, viewing reason as the most fundamental and rudimentary element of man. However the search for the unique nature of man does not end here. There are philosophers who contest this conviction and believe that the search for the unique element of man is not so simple. Jacques Maritan in his essay "Subject and Suppositum" opines that one of the reasons why this knowledge remains yet to be developed is that:

> the persons knowledge of the other persons differs essentially from the knowldege he has of himself. Others

> he knows as objects rather than as subjects, but himself he knows as subject and not as an object. In both the cases the knowledge of the subject is obscured, either totally or relatively.[1]

At other times the concept of 'person', 'self', or the 'real me', is frequently taken for granted as a metaphysical ultimate, i.e., as a primitive term or entity which cannot be reduced to or analysed into anything simpler. *Vis a vis* the body is taken to be neither ultimate nor simple, but something as merely composed of familiar chemical elements. But questions such as "am I the same as my body or is it that I who have a body?" often arise. However, note that the question is not 'who am I?' but 'what am I?' There is clearly a strong sense in which I am not the same as or identical with my body. This insight has been expressed in a multitude of ways: "The spirit is willing but the flesh is weak", "You bury only my body not me."

For the present, keeping these notions aside, let us take a look at the concept of man viewed earlier at some point of time.

1. *The Rationalistic View*: A view suggesting that what distinguishes man is the fact that he is a rational being. Philosophers like Plato and Aristotle held the supremacy of reason, the highest faculty of the soul. Mind is here understood to be the unifying and the organising principle and as such differs from the body. Contemporary American philosopher Ayn Rand too, extending the Aristotelian injunction speaks of reason as a faculty which

> is fundamental of human nature, because man is the organism who survives by its use. The mind is indispensable to human life, abstractions are not luxury but a necessity. Thought is man's guide to action.[2]

2. *The Judaeo-Christian View*: A perspective which understands man to be primarily as having a diving origin, i.e., his uniqueness lies not in the fact that he is rational animal, but as being related to god or as being created by him or in his image. This view is basically a theological or religious in its emphasis.

---

1. *A Modern Introduction to Metaphysics*, 1962.
2. *Objectivism*: *The Philosophy of Ayn Rand*, 1991.

3. *The Naturalistic View*: This views man as a part of the physical order of nature and one who is subject to the physical and chemical laws as are other organisms. A creature determined by the forces of nature and by his biological impulses, nevertheless having the capacity to transcend and manipulate the natural processes. In referring to this elements in the nature of man Reinhold Niebuhr remarks:

> to the essential nature of man belong on the one hand, all his natural endowments and determinations, his physical and social impulses, his sexual and racial diffentiation, in short his character as a creature embedded in the natural order. On the other hand, his essential also includes the freedom of his spirit, his transcendence over natural process, and finally his self-transcendence.[3]

However Rand disagrees on this thesis and insists that "man is not a battlefield of contending dimensions, spiritual and physical". But rather

> an indivisible entity, an integrated unit of two attributes of matter and consciousness. Consciousness in his case takes the form of mind and matter a certain kind of organic structure. Each of these attributes is indispensable to the other and to the total entity. The mind acquires knowledge and defines goals, the body translates these conclusion into action.[4]

Beside these perspectives we have yet another view that looks at man as a unity of the following four faculties or the 'self' as constituting of the four dimensions:

1. The cognitive (the ability of being self-conscious, reflective thinking, abstract thought, the power to generalise).
2. The emotive (the ability to make ethical discriminations).
3. The aesthetic (the ability of appreciation and the possessor

---

3. "The Nature and Destiny of Man", N.Y: Scribner's, 1941, I, *Human Nature*, p. 270.
4. In *Objectivism: The Philosophy of Ayn Rand*, 1991.

of creative mind).

4. The conative aspects (mostly said to be the active side of the human personality where in one is desiring, striving, willing and in all being able to make a choice or exercising the freedom of choice).

Sifting the Characteristic Properties of Man

These essential and distinguishing aspects of man has been disclosed by the human history past and present. However, though the human aspects such as feeling, believing, aspiring, hoping, etc., may be irrelevant to a strictly scientific approach, are very much central to our lives. Strawson is one of the philosophers who has greatly emphasised the notion of person. Strawson does not present a thesis or a linguistic clarification of the concept of person though he starts the essay "Persons" by listing some of the attributes that we often ascribe to ourselves or rather ways in which we think of ourselves.

Generally speaking we usually ascribe actions and intentions to ourselves for instance 'I am going to school', 'I shall go to the doctor tomorrow', etc. We also ascribe to ourselves sensations, e.g., 'I am in pain', perception, e.g., 'I see that the book is on the table', memories, e.g., 'I remember that I saw him at the station', location, e.g., 'I am in my room', etc. We also ascribe to ourselves attributes which are characteristically physical in nature such as height, weight, shape, colour, etc., kind of attributes that we also predicate to other objects unlike attributes such as memory, sensation, perception, intention, action, etc., which can be ascribed only to ourselves. What one is looking for in identifying a man is

> not a set of specific abilities like thinking or cooking — for then idiots and children would not be humans, but a single power which is the source of these diverse abilities.[5]

These instances show that the distinction between the application of attributes is 'specie-specific' and thus rests on the kind of objects that is in question. 'Man' is an object as is any animal to a scientist,

---

5. *The Range of Philosophy*, 1970.

is the sense that both are part of the physical order of nature, and man too is subject to the physical and the chemical laws as are other organisms. However he is a different kind of object in the sense that though he is determined by the forces of nature and by biological impulses, he has the capacity to transcend these natural processes or to manipulate them unlike other objects. As a person, man is to some extent free from the limitations that hold for the inorganic and the merely organic but un-self-conscious existing organisms. But what do we mean by 'free'? Besides, what kind of limitations are we talking about? Limitations could either mean that the organism itself is deficient of some necessary requirement or it could be the external limitation. However the first sense of limitation is basically a natural deformity which man, with his laborious efforts in the field of science and technology has tried to overcome, an obvious impossibility in case of the lower level organisms. And as far as the second notion of limitations is concerned, it has to be shown on what basis does man overcome certain external limitations which other organisms cannot. At a later point we will see as to why the elucidation of the concept of freedom is important and is at the same time one of the important aspects of man's nature.

I understand freedom to be comprehensible in two senses: One is being able to do what he can with the help of his 'physical constitution'. 'Free' in this sense is being able to use his potentialities and skills. The other is to choose from certain alternatives and plan his course of action accordingly. 'Free' in this sense means being able to act on the basis of his 'moral constitution'. The first will enable him to overcome the external forces that cloud his goals and the second which enables him to choose between alternatives that will be socially conducive and acceptable.

A general understanding of 'freedom' suggests an absence of any kind of compulsion or force that would influence or modify the end result. Let us illustrate. A fish for instance in an aquarium is forced to survive on the foodgrains that is provided to it, and it will be out of its capacity to get food for itself the day it does not get. On the other hand, the same fish if it is kept in a pond, will definitely not have to be dependent on the foodgrains that will be provided to it but can fetch for itself somehow or the other in the pond. But, if by chance there is no food for this fish in the pond itself it will die, since it cannot ever go out of the pond to get its food. Unlike this and other such organisms, man on the other hand, is capable of overcoming certain barriers and doing what is required. A classic case which would prominently highlight this point is the making of a weapon. To survive, man had to kill animals and to do that he had to invent some method by which he could kill them. As a result he invented a technique, a weapon that would fulfil this purpose. Similarly, everytime he faced some difficulty, he was able to overcome it. He is, in this sense, able to manipulate the conditions in which he is put and to achieve his needs and goals by way of using his potentialities and skills. In this sense freedom is the 'ability to do' that which would get rid of the obstacles or being able to manipulate or modify the external circumstances, and what enables man to overcome this hurdles is his use reason. We shall come to this point a little later and for the present see how man is free in the second sense.

Man being a social animal has to follow some norms of the society which are incorporated by the inhabitants of the society so as to preserve harmony and peace in the society. Various laws like the legal, the moral, the cultural, the religious, institutional laws, etc., are enforced to assure harmony in the society. These laws seem to impose tremendous restrictions on man which forces him to act according to them. Thus man's action in this context, strictly speaking, can be said to be either 'obedience' or 'disobedience' to these laws. However, the case is not so watertight since we often see, that alternatives are always present and man has a choice either to take it or choose some other alternative. There is no law that restricts this freedom of choice. No one dictates him the kind of alternative he has to choose. The only thing that is not within his reach is the alternatives that are not placed before him. For instance let us take the case of euthanasia. Medical law as well as legal law considers it to be wrong to take anybody's life. However keeping certain conditions and situations in mind like the fact that the patient is terminally ill and there are no chances of his recovery, there are only two alternatives: either to give consent and withdraw the artificial life supporting systems or let the patient die a painful death. Here the choice will be made keeping in mind the moral side of the case too and whatever decision that will follow will be based on some reasons. The choice made under this situation will be said to be a rational choice. Thus, making a wise choice from the available alternatives is yet another manifestation of man's use of reason.

At this junctions, it seems important that we understand what we mean by use of reason or a man being a rational animal, and why this has to set him apart from the rest of the organisms?

The platform on which a man can be distinguished from other organisms, views Rand, is on "the basis of the means of survival" (*Objectivism: The Philosophy of Ayn Rand*, 1991). To illustrate the point take a look at the way the plants which survive by the means of physical function: of acquiring food, sunlight, water, etc., from the soil and air in which they grow, however, minus the need of the awareness that they need so. Animals, on the other hand, who can be said to be species of lower consciousness apparently have the faculty of sensations and the ability to learn a set of vital skills like hunting, storing food, building nest, etc., essential for their survival. Man's ability to reason besides the power to perceive and experience through the senses along with the different kinds of abilities vital for his survival, is what makes his survival possible and sets him above the rest of the organisms. What is suggested is that, he and nobody beside him is gifted with this tool 'to reason', and that he is not merely a stimulus responding organism, a product of conditioned reflexes or instincts unlike other organism which act on instincts or impulses, or id reflexes, actions elicited unconsciously. The actions of man on the other hand are chosen and desired as we have seen earlier are the product of reason. Reason provides him with the pros and cons of the choice that he should make, thus helping him to choose the required course of action.

But how do we understand and comprehend this notion of reason on which most of our actions and choices is based? If a definition is all that we require, then we can have it right from the neurologists to the psychologists giving definitions, but this is not what we are seeking. Let us, however, not dabble into the various kinds of answers given to this question, but attempt to fix at least one lucid and simple answer which can be easily comprehended. As is said earlier, based on the notion of ability we pointed out that humans can perform skills of a higher order than other animate objects because they have this faculty of reason. We also observe astonishing skill such as creating a piece of music, sculpturing, playing games, use of language, writing computer programmes, doing mathematics, etc., that support the claim that all this is made possible only through reason or the use of his cognitive faculty. Thus the power to reason marks not only the peculiarity and uniqueness of the human specie but also reveals his distinguishing and elusive nature by means of performing astounding skills. But the question that comes to our mind is: what is it about this cognitive faculty that makes all this possible? What sort of mechanism is responsible for these kinds of actions. As an explanation to this we have the scientific, the psychological, the neurological, the sociological and many more significant points of view are available. But, looking at the present context, a philosophical approach is what we need. Let us consider this issue in brief.

Sensations and perceptions are said to be providing the data, the basic material on which an individual builds his conceptual systems. Organisms of lower level consciousness are, as is said earlier, merely stimuli responding. They do not further this material or data. Their correlation with the reality is limited and restricted, because they are not equipped with the tool to improve upon anything given within their ambiance. Human beings on the other hand are equipped with the tool of reason that helps him to manipulate, improve or modify the material that he receives from senses, perceptions of his surroundings. They have this ability of not only organising and classifying the data that they get, but also the ability to integrate these data into a coherent whole, the ability with which he can generalise the given data by virtue of his power (the power of the cognitive faculty) to condense the sensory information. In other words, the human being is one who can perceive, organise, abstract, integrate and connect the material he receives. And the way he goes about in connecting, organising and generalising the data is by the use of logic. Let us illustrate.

When we say that a candle cannot solve a mathematical problem but the rational man can, what are we hinting at? It is just saying that one is unable to solve while the other is, but why is it so? Let us attempt to resolve this by first answering what does it take to solve a mathematical problem? Firstly one need to understand the symbols, what they stand for, how they function, and the rules to manipulate these symbols. Beside all these it is also essential that one grasps the meaning of all this and the way to go about using rules in a logical way. However, having the material is not sufficient, one has to manipulate it in such a way that it achieves or reaches the set target. This can be said to the plants too that to produce chlorophyll is similar to this, that the material is given and when the mechanism is activated, which means that it has manipulated the material, it is able to reach its target: producing chlorophyll. However, the only difference between these two is that while human beings can do *the same things in numerous way* and with some scope of error the latter cannot and there will never be any error, all that we can say in case something goes wrong and it dies, it is because of uncondusive conditions. Thus in case of plants it can be said that to produce chlorophyll is the ability of the plant, but that it is green is its property.

Thus, while saying that something is a property is to say that the object is predisposed with it and hence classified on identification of similar property in other objects. Similarly in the case of human beings, it is its property to be a rational being, one which they are predisposed with. However to say that a plant is green because it produces chlorophyll or that because it produces chlorophyll it is green, is similar to saying that because man is rational he can solve a mathematical problem or that because he can solve a mathematical problem he is rational. Thus to reason is the property of a man while to show such competence in solving a mathematical problem is his ability which is unquestionably a product of his reason. The epitomisation of this claim is well summarised by Ayn Rand in "Fountainhead" wherein she says

> from the simplest necessity to the highest abstraction, from the wheel to the skyscraper, everything we are and everything we have comes from a single attribute of man — the function of his reasoning mind.

Conclusion

I would like to conclude this essay by summarising Ayn Rand's view of man:

> Man is the opposite of the feeble creature imagined by the religionists and behaviourists alike. He is not a palsied atom to be pitied or manipulated, but an autonomous entity to be respected and admired — on one condition: If he earns his respect by his choices. It applies to every individual with a rational faculty.

That this faculty of his not only determines the choices he has and will make but also his character and thereby his life. In this sense man is said to be self-created, self-directed and self-responsible. Thus 'man' is one who chooses his own ends and the methods that he will use to attain them. All this suggest only one thing that by virtue of his metaphysical nature he is not a pawn of forces beyond his control. He can surpass all the difficulties that come his way by the use of his cognitive faculty. Thus the cognitive faculty of man is 'specie-specific' as we have observed by way of our discusion and it will definitely lead to a category mistake if we attribute to non-human beings.

A Vedāntic Model of Spiritual Humanism

Subhas E. Bhelkey

MAN is being understood in various ways. There are several qualities of man which distinguish him from other animals. Such differentiation is done in contexts and many times the differentiations are not logically strict and even then they highlight man's difference or uniqueness in the animal kingdom. One of such descriptions of man, presented by Aristotle is that man is a rational animal. He wanted to highlight the human capacity of reasoning in abstraction and recursively. Such a description makes us to think further that man develops logic and follows a logical way in his behaviour. A certain logical way can be easily traced in the behaviour of many other animals. But the artificiality, deliberateness and recursiveness make human reason and logicality different from that of other animals. The credit of human progress largely goes to man's rationality. Nevertheless it is a fact that the same reason has brought several calamities to man in his individual and social life. Many times it so happens because there is no proportion of and balance between the two aspects of human personality, viz., rational and emotional or sentimental. An excess of anyone invites problems. And man does go on inviting problems continuously. This is the reason why man acquires another description which is unique, viz., that man is a problem-solving animal. Personally, I would prefer to characterise man not as a problem-solving animal but problem-creating animal, since most of the problems in the human world are human problems rather than natural calamities.

A man is capable of creating problems because he can interact with other humans and objects in the world. If all were mechanical,

I wonder whether there would be any problem, any challenge, any scope to human reason to overcome it and prove the uniqueness of his identity. In fact, the sourcc of human problem lies in man himself and that is something unique about man and his world. Man could establish himself as a significant creature in the universe because he has been reacting and responding to the problems and challenges posed by himself. This leads us to reveal another significant aspect of human nature that man is a creative animal. In order to solve the problem and overcome the problematic situation, man creates his own structures as the building blocks of his universe. To satisfy his insatiable wants he creates a world for enjoyment. Every rise and satisfaction of man's desire leaves an impact on him which further programmes his personality to repeat and repeat again the same course. This is how his needs turn into wants and his satisfaction opens an unreachable horizon of cravings. This puts a challenge to him and in response he creates a world in which he seeks satisfaction of his insatiable wants. When he realises the futility of such a mode of living it puts before him another challenge to conquer over the craving and desires. This, too, leads to the creation of a world in which he can terminate his journey of consumption and enjoyment.

Such a widespread picture of human nature confuses us to locate the essence which can describe properly his uniqueness. Nevertheless, one aspect of his nature seems more prominent in all human endeavours. In all efforts man tries to be more and more articulate. Man has a capacity to know and learn. He goes much beyond just an experience and knows about the object. He has a capacity to make his sensations more and more distinct so that he can reach up to the essence of an object. When he makes his sensations more and more distinct, he knows the object and when he reaches to the essence, he knows the object completely. In order to make the sensations distinct he uses various skills. He eliminates some parts and joins with it some other parts. This is how he goes on articulating in which he creates abstract structures. He has a capacity to eliminate and join various elements of sensations obtained in experience. It begins with single objects and continues with a multitude of complex objects. He carries out the basic structure of an object by abstracting the superfluous parts and further constructs a complex structure of many such basic units. Thus, given in his experience, he makes his sensations distinct and then goes on associating and dissociating the obtained elements the way he thinks or imagines having them in a complex structure. This is the basic architecture of his creativity. This architecture reveals a very important aspect of human capacity that it can either make the latent structures more and more vivid or construct the imagined designs by rearranging them. A man who can reveal the essence and the structure of an object can very well conceal the same by the use of his skill of rearrangement. When man makes the essential part distinct, he uses the gestalt technique for separating and lifting up some part as foreground leaving the other on the background. Man knows an object and learns to know more and other objects. In knowing man reveals and also conceals. He further learns to reveal and conceal other objects. The same skill is used for concealing the nature of an object. As man conceals the nature of objects he deals with, he conceals his own nature cunningly. When we learn something new, when the true nature of something gets revealed to us, it happens suddenly just like magic. The same technique can be repeated, but now not in happening but in performing. Man knows and learns the suddenness of revelation and repeats it in concealment. To reveal is human because of certain skills and the same skills lead to conceal. In revelation the latent are made manifest and in concealment the essence is hidden behind the new arrangement.

The early form of learning is seen in imitation or mimicry. This is seen as a natural tendency in man right from his childhood. This tendency makes man mischievous. It is noticed that man takes more pleasure in mimicry. As man develops his personality, he also acts and performs a role different from his own nature and makes others to believe it as his own nature. The capacity in man to present himself or any object as it is and also differently is astonishing. Both of his activities — revelation and concealment — are preceded by deliberation and contemplation. If he deceives, he deceives deliberately and if he is cunning, he is cunning deliberately. He knows what he does and he is aware why and how does he do it.

Man is great because of his achievements. His achievements are seen in his creations. When he creates, he establishes an order in the world of his creations. For establishing an order he formulates some rules and follows them. In order to make rules man has to reveal the modes in which the various patterns of a structure are functioning. Man develops an insight not only into the structure of an object but also into the mode of functioning and operations which take place in the case of natural or artificial happenings. He knows the principles behind operations and functioning, he learns them to practice and accordingly follows them. He follows the rules, not only of the natural happenings but also of the human world. He makes the rules deliberately and follows them deliberately. He makes and follows the rules not because he is helpless and bound to do so but because he is capable of breaking rules. It is maintained since long that man is a rule-making animal. This reveals his creativity, rationality, discipline, deliberateness, articulation and adoption. However, I feel that the better description of man revealing his uniqueness would be that man is a rule-breaking or rule-violating animal. It is deliberately that he breaks rules and even then compensates the loss or damage which takes place due to violating rules. He has carved out his way and he can deviate from the way he has already set. When he deviates from the way, he can reach the goal in spite of it or he can choose deliberately to reach some other goal. Nevertheless, he violates rules and he violates them because he enjoys it. Making the rules and following the rules satisfies man but violating the rules gives man pleasure as he enjoys it. In fact, one of the avenues he has found to get joy in life is through violating the rules. Several times he breaks rules not because he wants to disturb the order or harm any regulated course, but because he enjoys it. He enjoys in it a challenge, an adventure, a novelty and uncertainty. He follows a deviation as a challenge to his creativity and problem-solving ability. He enjoys an adventurous expedition which involves uncertainty, poses the threats of failure and incompleteness. Every expedition reveals before him something new. In his creative attitude he goes on searching for alternatives in the realm of infinite possibilities. In his endeavour he improves, modifies and changes previous rules. The development of sciences seems to have behind it an ulterior motive to break the rules. It is said that a person is good because he obeys — obeys rules and laws. A disobedient person is usually unaccepted in a society. Perhaps a man may be disobedient to find out for himself whether he can obey.

And a person like Mahatma Gandhi may give a call to the people to disobey the government to get dignity for themselves. When one disobeys, one deviates from the given rule but follows some other rule. So, even in disobedience there is a respect for obedience on a higher order and in violating rules, there is following a rule. In a way, man is continuously searching for revelation — revelation of the nature of the object before him, of the world, of his own nature and of the course of his mode of living. In this search he makes rules, follows rules, breaks rules, violates rules, modifies rules, but ultimately reveals his nature and a path to reach it which can give him satisfaction of completeness.

A man who is set for an adventurous expedition of revelation has to look back to his own nature. What is the field through which his road of expedition will pass? And what is the final goal where his expedition will terminate with full satisfaction? Although it is true that man strives for pleasure, prosperity, development and progress in his life, that does not become the final goal in his life. He has evolved several structures — social, political, economic, cultural, religious, etc., for the achievement of his material goals. Still something remains to be done and achieved in life. These are the realms in which he creates the structures, institutions and systems. And the same later on poses challenge to his humanity. Man creates them to use for his purpose and he also misuses them out of his selfish and egoistic motives. This is the point where he creates a problem for himself by allowing all these systems to turn inhuman. Hence, it becomes necessary to think of such a form where the scope to his misuse of mischief will be minimised and his intentions will be pure. It is in the ideal of the spiritual humanism that we can get an assurance to overcome the limitations of human nature and pursue the journey ahead.

One of the most notorious words and hence the concepts has been that of a spirit or spiritual in the Indian context. With the advent of indology there has been not only translation but also Westernisation of Indian texts and conepts which took place in a large scale. Indian texts and hence the tradition was introduced and exposed to the west through the Western languages and the categories or Western culture. The concepts like religion, spirit are some of those concepts which do not have proper belongings in the

Indian tradition but are now well implanted in Indian languages and minds. The term 'spiritual humanism' may have a specific meaning in the Western tradition. In the Indian tradition, however, we have to first locate the proper bearing for this notion and then think about its plausibility.

Usually the term spiritual is used in the Indian context which is otherwise called as *ādhyātmika*. *Adhyātma* means that which pertains to *ātman*. *Ātman* in Upaniṣadic metaphysics is taken as the reality in its essence. Sometimes it refers to the reality or the ontic essence demarcated by an individual person or sometimes by the entire cosmos. It being the reality existing in its own right, it is also taken as transcendent in nature. The texture of this existence differs from the texture of the existence of objects which are known to us by our sense-organs. This may make one to use the word spirit in this context and some scholars have treated *ātman* as spirit or that which pertains to *ātman* as spiritual.

In the Indian tradition, *adhyātma* presupposes a certain point of view, not only to understand the world but also to live life. It refers to the position of a realised person. According to Advaita Vedānta one knows the nature of the ultimate reality, viz., *Brahman* as it is and knowing the *Brahman* culminates into becoming one with the *Brahman — brahma vid brahmaiva bhavati*, or *nā'ham asmi brahmaiva asti iti pratiyat*. This Advaitic metaphysics has many serious implications. Advaita Vedānta does not deny the life or an ordianry person, nor does it deny the life of a realised person. According to Advaita, then, living life in society is meaningful and such a life is inevitable for every man who lives in society. A man, whether completely realised and hence liberated or not yet liberated is given to understand that everything is *Brahman* and *Brahman* is everywhere. Essentially it is the same *ātman* which belongs to or pervades into all beings, though there is differentiations due to different personal identities of different beings. This difference may have any purpose, but certainly it is not meant for anybody to discriminate them. What is to be seen and stressed is the essential sameness amongst all beings. This position gives a vision of which one can develop a social philosophy and that social philosophy could be humanistic in nature. Such a point of view, developed especially by Advaita Vedānta, gives us a model of humanistic thought and since it is based on the principles of the nature and knowing the *ātman* it is *ādhyātmika* in nature, it is a form of spiritual humanism.

The first characterisation of spiritual humanism is that it goes beyond the considerations of any caste, creed and religion. Since it pertains to *ātman*, it is transcendent in nature and being transcendent it overcomes shortcomings of all sectarian and relative views. In fact, in the West a significant movement of humanism arose as a reaction to the domination of religion. Humanism basically gives stress on establishing the dignity of man. The Protagorean principle is operative behind it which holds that man is the measure of all things. Man knows the world and he knows through his, i.e., human categories. Although man is subjected to the laws of nature, he is not a slave of nature. He enjoys full freedom as a creature of nature. He follows the laws of nature but also tries to make use of those laws for his own purpose. Like the natural world there is imagined another world, the world of religion which may be very good and useful for man's development and happiness. However, it turns tyrannical. Many of the religious institutions, norms, practices and rituals ruthlessly subjugate man under the fear of some unseen and supernatural powers. Instead of reverence and surrender it takes the hold of the feeling of fear in man. Instead of nourishing self-respect and dignity in man it nourishes guilt and condemnation. Against this form of religion, humanism arose in the guise of a revolt. It does not insist any rule of an ideology or doctrine. It believes in giving freedom to man on all levels. All men are free. All men are equal. Neither any agency exterior to humans nor any single human being is expected to rule men. The perspective given by humanism, in this way, establishes the dignity of man. In order to preserve the dignity of man the freedom of man should be preserved. Although man lives in society and aspires for the attainments of his personal and social goals, he is not constrained by any individual or institution. All are free and in this respect all are equal. At the same time the goal of human life is to preserve the humanness in the world. In order to preserve such a humanness, he has to behave in a human way without losing the human face. If such a mode of life is to be followed in totality and successfully, the desirable form appears to be that of a spiritual humanism and we get a practicable variety of spiritual humanism in the Advaitic way of life.

It is necessary to refer to some concrete proposal as far as the Advaitic mode of spiritual humanism is concerned. I would like to present here a case that in one of the small poetic compositions, Śaṅkarācārya has described the ideal form of spiritual humanism. The composition is a praise in the name of Lord Viṣṇu. It is called as *Śatpadīstotra*. It must be noted, first, that this composition is made in the praise of the lord and we are using and interpreting it as a model for spiritual humanism. Hence, we shall treat some of the terms and concepts symbolically and fit them in our context of spiritual humanism. This composition is a prayer of the Lord Viṣṇu to request him to bring about those desirable changes in an ordinary man who aspires to lead good and happy life. Here the author does not directly preach any transcendence of an ordinary life. A man lives in a society and he has to continue to live in a society so that his personal goals will be achieved in the pursuance of the achievement of the social goals. Here the author accepts the order of the highest lord and even then retains the humanness of human life.

The problem in human life is due to man's attitude towards the other — where the other may be a human being or an animal or anything as such or the society at large of the world as a whole. When there is rise and fixation of an ego and an attempt to fix the ego for identification, the responses of man towards the other change. Man turns tyrannical in such a situation which develops an inhuman attitude. Even if a man is aware of the ultimate truth of life he constantly needs reminders to remain in a serene state of mind and maintain the balanced position. What is required to regulate in this situation is to develop modesty and humility. It is prayed and requested that the attitude of arrogance should be removed. The egoist is arrogant and in his arrogant attitude he turns aggressive. It is the aggressiveness which makes the whole discourse inhuman and behind this aggressiveness there is arrogance. When the religion goes in the hands of those who are or become arrogant, religion becomes inhuman. Similar is the case of science and technology. When the executing person uses the system for his personal glorification, the whole system becomes inhuman and then there is a call of humanism. In the case of spiritual humanism, however, there are less chances of turning the discourse inhuman, since it is based on the understanding of one's own nature on the one hand and the nature of the reality on the other hand. Such an understanding does make the person modest and humble.

What are the reasons due to which man turns arrogant and becomes aggressive? It is the unregulated mind, uncontrolled passions and insatiable desires which make man self-centred and egoist. Religion *qua* religion is never bad, science *qua* science is never bad, modernisation *qua* modernisation, too, is never bad. The man operates them is having certain motives and when his motives are irregular and erratic, they do harm to humanity. Hence, what is required is a control and regulation of man's mind, passions and desires. Human mind can be regulated and disciplined not by depriving it from its natural objects of consumption but by allowing it to satisfy in it natural course with the minimum natural requirement. Human mind is not to be repressed, but it is to be trained and regulated. Śaṅkarācārya says in his composition that the mind is to be controlled and regulated. There are several desires and wants. All of them are not genuine. With a rigorous exercise of discrimination the genuine desires are to be identified and allowed to get satisfied, but not to be allowed to increase in an improportionate and excessive way. There are several desires which are futile, which can be never satisfied. They are like a mirage. Such desires are to be calmed down. Man may get involved in the objects of satisfaction related to his senses. But he has to overcome this course of life. This is overcoming one's own self, this is coming out of the shackles of egotism. When one thus overcomes one's limited personality, one lives the life not for oneself but for the others. When the mind is not directed to one's own mind, when there are no passions controlling one's life, one enters into a wider field — the infinite realm of the social self or the 'general will'. The will is no more restricted to a particular individual or an ego but has pervaded over the endless extent of the social self. In this state of consciousness, man's awareness is oriented towards the good for the all — the entire society. This is the stage when one overcomes one's ego and limitedness of oneself, there emerges the feeling of compassion in one's mind. The feeling of self-love is basically pertaining to the mundane life, it is worldly or this worldly, it is rooted into passions and desires, it is limited and restricted to the boundaries of an individual self. But when the self elevates itself due to the higher understanding of the nature of the self and reality the self-love transforms into compassion. The feeling of compassion is something 'spiritual', it pertains to the domain of *ātman*. To develop a compassion for the other, i.e., for each and every being — living or non-living — is a spiritual development of man which overcomes all sorts of hierarchies and discriminations amongst human beings. The perfect human attitude will be found in this awareness which is filled with nothing else but compassion for the other. Any life lived with this awareness will be an ideal example of humanism; and this is a case of a spiritual humanism. Śaṅkarācārya says that this feeling of compassion is natural to man and hence is present in every man. But what is required is to develop that feeling in such a way that the entire life will get pervaded by it. What we need is an expansion of this compassion in our life. And this is the way to overcome the hurdles of limitedness, bondage, miseries and calamities which is the real challenge before man. Man finds difficult to live his life due to several obstacles and oppositions in the way to reach his goals in his life to get satisfaction and completeness. The correct solution is to live the life motivated fully by compassion and not by self-love. When man becomes aware of his spiritual unity and integrity, he lives the life of compassion. When he realises the true nature of the *ātman* and further realises that the same *ātman* is pervading and present in the entire universe including all its beings, he leads the life of a true humanist. The spiritual humanism, thus, is an awareness of one's spiritual integrity and living the life accordingly. Whatever are the problems of failure, dissatisfaction, lamentation, sufferings, miseries either in indivudual life or in social life, can be overcome by following the spiritual humanism which maintains the essential unity or the *ātman* in the entire universe. This is to be seen from the point of view of living the life which involves all sorts of actions, interactions, performances and doings. Spiritual humanism consists in living the same life but with the awareness of the higher understanding of the essential unity of the *ātman*. It does not preach any nihilistic or ascetic way of life to give up passions, desires and wants, but it preaches to live with the same passions, desires and wants but on the higher (or transcendent) level with the higher consciousness. According to this spiritual humanism the entire world is one community. It goes beyond all geographical and political boundaries in which the entire human race is divided. There are different races, different histories to each of them, different societies with different legacies. Nevertheless, all these races and societies have the same aspirations. This is realised when the essential unity of *ātman* is understood. This brings all men together and builds one homogeneous family of them under one roof. It is the spiritual humanism which can offer solutions to serious and pseudo problems the humanity is suffering from today.

Śaṅkarācārya reveals in this composition the root of the human problem. Man loses his balance and behaves in an uncontrolled manner because there is a fear rooted in him. He seems to be afraid of the challenges and hurdles he faces in his life to reach his goals successfully. He is afraid because he lacks confidence in himself. He is not certain about his capacities and achievements. This happens because he is not aware of himself — aware of his true nature and his potential *vis-a-vis* the reality. He lacks the understanding of unity of *ātman*. This makes him afraid of the task he has to perform in his life. Consequently he gets frustrated and becomes desperate. These are the true human problems. Śaṅkarācārya refers to them as the true concern of man. And the solution to them, again, he shows in the ideal of spiritual humanism. The spirituality in the sense of *ādhyātmika* in the Indian context does not mean other-worldliness or asceticism, but means living the normal social life for prosperity and peace with an outlook from the philosophical doctrine which reveals the nature of *ātman* and its relation with *Brahman*. This form of humanism transgresses the political and ideological differences and believes in the oneness of man, believes in the hope of man which is for man's prosperity, happiness and well-being. It presupposes love for the other and confidence in the other. It gives the due respect to man and his achievements and establishes his dignity. It moulds and moderates the egoism and aggressiveness into modesty and compassion which is based purely on human values and human considerations. It accepts that man is at the centre of all affairs and makes the man grow up to the level of the cosmos. Spirituality states the merger of an individual soul into the cosmic reality. But this merger does not turn totalitarian-spiritualism points of the true limits of man and humanness and at the same time it helps man to overcome those limits to live the satisfactory and meaningful life. It should be noted that the spirituality of the Indian spiritual humanism is a-religious. It does not require subjugation of a man before the supernatural. Rather it enables man to acquire new and better identity in the merger into the cosmic reality. Such a merger dignifies human existence by making an individual person to extend his love, compassion and modesty to include into it the entire humanity. It is a fact that man and the society are different and such a difference is real. But the relationship that holds between the man and society is such that man belongs to the society, society does not belong to man. This doctrine is explained with a metaphor that a wave in the sea belongs to the sea but the sea does not belong to a wave. A wave is known as a wave as it has been ascribed an independent existence. But the wave is an inseparable part emerged on the surface of the sea for a short while. The sea gives the way its existence, its grandeur and its beauty. The sea is always open to allow the wave to recede back and repose into the sea and for the next moment it supports the wave to raise, it holds the wave by keeping itself on the background. Neither the sea dissociate itself from the wave nor the wave dictates the sea. Waves do remain coming and going on the sea and the sea makes their existence possible. When man realises this relation between himself and society he gets the feeling of disgust about his own egoism, arrogance and aggressiveness. The correct way for successful achievements is not aggressiveness but it is modesty. The society is all powerful and living as a part of society helps to preserve the dignity of man. It also ensures justice to all, peace and happiness in the entire society. It does make any attempt to belittle man as an individual nor does it strip off man of his freedom, his choice, his discrimination and his satisfaction.

The real danger man has is from his arrogance. When he lacks confidence he gets filled with fear and to overcome such a fear he turns arrogant. This makes him to behave in an inhuman manner. Various social and political organisations, religious set-ups, when run by such men, they create a danger to man's humanity, i.e., man's dignity and freedom. An individual is insecure. When he individuates himself from the society, he loses all his strength and then gets affected by the fear-complex. The true savour of an individual is the society at large. He is secure when he belongs to society. And his humanity is meaningful till he belongs to the society. A faith in the creed that man is an inseparable part of society can provide security to him. This creed is a social form of the metaphysical doctrine of the *ādhyātmika* way of life according to which there is an essential unity between *ātman* and *Brahman*.

This Vedāntic model of spiritual humanism gives us a basic structure from which we can workout in details the various structures, institutions and systems which actually govern the social life.

What is the Language of Humanism?

Priyadarshi Patnaik

Why Talk of Language!

IN contemporary academics language is like a neurosis. Whatever we attempt to do traces itself back to the problem of language. We feel intensely that the world we live in is a socio-cultural construct based on certain concepts and categories, and that these categories and concepts can be traced back to language. Our acts, human or inhuman, our awareness of ourselves and our relation with our surrounding are all determined by the way we think about all these; and to think we use language. On the other hand, the common man, especially in a country like India, almost never thinks of language. Among the uneducated, language is unselfconscious. And in cities we live in a time which is constantly threated with change. In such a situation we hardly have time to think about anything. It is in this context that I feel it is important for us to try to think of the relation of language (or various modes of languaging) to the concept of Humanism.

Can I Mean Anything?

Today the language which we use in an academic circle is used with a great deal of care. In fact, certain historical processes like Structuralism, post-Structuralism and post-Modernism have at the present moment led to an acute awareness of the language we move in. Whether history or historicity is significant or whether history of everything including the language we use is dissolving into a post-Modern or contemporary amnesia is an open question. But we still have many words which have long histories and we move among their histories trying to ascertain our position.

These words, when we trace them back etymologically, were used to mean different things at different times. They are also used today differently by different schools, by different people. *Humanism* is one such word. Today language is no longer something which is self-contained — a common medium or a common cultural code. Since we now question the very validity of the convention of languaging, its stability and permanence, it eludes us.

After Ferdinand de Saussure's insightful exploration of language, no longer as a history, but as a system, we know that a language-specific culture or society *decides* that a certain word means a certain thing. In other words, the bond between words and what they mean is not something natural or essential but accidental. "The language we use is a convention, and it makes no difference what exactly the nature of the agreed sign is."[1] This scientific approach has had its repercussions on us. In looking at language as something outside of us whose structure can be analysed and certain general rules drawn, we have managed to alienate language from us. "The language itself is not a function of the speaker. It is the product passively registered by the individual."[2] The voice that speaks, the letter that one reads are only *symptoms* of a language system, individual cases, and are known as *parole*. A culture specific language is *langue*. The universal human phenomenon of communication through certain modes is *language.*[3] Thus, our very way of looking at language is reversed, Language as a structured system is "... the social part of language, external to the individual who by himself is powerless either to create or to modify it."[4] Language used to live within us. As *authors* we used to generate it and then regulate it with full authority. Now we live within it. It uses us as we used to use it. It has a life apart from us, beyond us, with its own moods and caprices. This extreme position came with

---

1. Ferdinand de Saussure, "Object of Study", in *Modern Criticism and Theory: A Reader,* ed. by David Lodge, Longman, London, 1998, p. 4.
2. *Ibid.*, p. 7.
3. *Ibid.*
4. *Ibid.*

the realisation that the bond between word and concept (meaning) is not something stable. Saussure talked of the bond between the signifier and the signified (broadly articulated sound pattern and the concept it refers to). But a closer look suggested that word and meaning were not something that formed a permanent bond. The relation between them was a working relation, always contingent to variations and changes. In other words, the signifier and the signified form two planes than constantly slide over one another. If we look at the history of each word, it has meant different things at different times, it has meant many things at the same time, it also can mean different things to different people simultaneously.

All this became somewhat evident after Jacquies Derrida's seminal paper, "Structure, Sign and Play" where he questioned the very basis of any philosophical or scientific position — the possibility of a stable centre which regulates the entire structure which is built upon it while itself being stable and beyond question. Each such position is based on *a priori* — something which cannot be questioned within that discourse or system of discourse. But Derrida showed that if one looked closer one found within the same discourse elements which contradicted the centre, *a priori* or the axiom. In other words, each discourse contained within it the potential for its own destruction or deconstruction.[5]

Looking at *Humanism* today implies looking at the word with all this awareness. Additionally, it means looking at the word *Humanism* through language in which it lives and from which it has emerged and evolved.

We have expressions such as Scientific Humanism, Marxist Humanism, Liberal Humanism, Existential Humanism and so on. If two scholars are asked to define any of the above terms they will, in all probabilities, come up with two widely different definitions for each of them. This does not mean that any attempt at definition is futile. It also does not mean the extreme position that although using the same articulation or signifier or sound pattern they mean two different things. If we take any of these stands, which much of

---

5. Jacquies Derrida, "Structure, Sign and Play in the Discourses of Human Sciences", in *Modern Criticism*.

modern literary theory leads towards, we can only encounter an uneasy silence — the residue of a language which has broken down.

During the greater part of the eighteenth and the nineteenth century in Europe, the writer was given a great deal of importance. The concept of property with all its legal implications had already made itself strongly felt.[6] And royalty, for a popular writer, was becoming a normal practice — something which was non-existent in the Renaissance Europe. In the fifteenth and the sixteenth-century Europe anybody could print a play or modify it or even claim it as his own with a few changes. Plagiarism was normal and an accepted norm as it is in today's post-Modern art and music. But by the nineteenth century the bond between the writer and his text was considered sacred. The text was legally sanctioned as the writer's property. Language was now not only a medium for business, it was business itself, coming as a tightly knit bundle of words — the text.

In this over-emphasis on the relation between the writer and his printed words, the reader was neglected and found himself in a signification system where he functioned almost passively. The reaction to this in the twentieth century, especially in Foucault and later Barthes, was what perhaps lead to another extreme position — that and the fact that property and ownership had and still have certain capitalistic implications.

As long as we speak of the bond between an author and his work, we are constrained by social conventions. We have to limit our interpretation or understanding of the text in the light of his words about his work, the relation of this particular text to other texts written by him, and also by his personal life. In other words, the author is not a mere name attached to the text, he is also a history, an imposition on the text which is modified by all these. The text is strongly linked to an *individual*, his history, his memory. A specific *human being* in his relation to a chain of words is again and again being re-emphasised. In an extreme attack on this overemphasis on the relation of an author and his work Michael Foucault reduced the author to a function — he is no longer asserted as an individual,

---

6. Michael Foucault, "What is an Author", in *Modern Criticism*.

as a human being but is reduced to a conventional component in the language system. The author is:

> a certain functional principle by which, in our culture, one limits, excludes, and chooses; in short, by which one impedes the free circulation, the free manipulation, the free composition, decomposition, and recomposition of fiction.[7]

The positions that evolved were ones where the reader in his relation to the text was overemphasised as the writer had once been. Roland Barthes, affirming this position in his "The Death of the Author" says that a text's unity lies not in its origin, but in his destination—the reader.[8] Interpretation attained great significance with the greater freedom of the reader. The reader need not necessarily understand what the writer intends to mean. In fact, it is not possible to know what the writer means, nor is it necessary — the writer is now out of fashion. All we have is the text. But even as we look at the text, we find that the same words can mean so many different things. 'Work' can mean reading, talking over the phone, running and so on. There is no way of verifying this since text is the only reality they refer to, i.e., it is a self-referential world. And with concepts, say Humanism, things become even more difficult. Now that the reader can flout the socio-cultural restraints imposed upon his interpretation, he can interpret it any way he wishes. Texts, from a writer's points of view, can be mutilated, manipulated, mis-read in a world where all readings can only be 'misreading'.[9]

This leaves us with the reader. But what is a reader? What is the nature of the *destination* to which a text must finally go? (This) destination can no longer be personal: the reader is without history, biography, psychology; his is simply that someone who holds together in a single field all the traces by which the written text is constituted.[10]

---

7. Michael Foucault, p. 209.
8. Ronald Barthes, "Death of the Author", in *The Rustle of Language*, Basil Blackwell, London, 1986, p. 117.
9. Harold Bloom, *A Map of Misreading*, Oxford University Press, New York, 1975, p. 3.
10. Ronald Barthes, "Death of the Author", p. 171.

Where does this lead us?

1. The author as an individual, as a subjective entity, even as a concept, is dead.

2. The reader, whose freedom initially fascinates us is only an anonymous subjectivity, an unnamed consciousness that processes texts and fabricates more texts.

3. The human being, the individual, is threatened with obliteration. If he exists at all, he exists as mere impersonal functionality.

What am I in a Mass?

The points which I have mentioned above do not apply only to a person who is deeply aware of language and culture. The common man, the *mass* man, is also significantly affected whether he is aware of it or not. But what is a mass man?

A mass man, as I understand it, is a man who is not taken into account for what he is, but as an *unit* of the mass. He is statistical quantity, he is in fact a metonymic creation, where a part is substituted for the whole.

Mass man, mass media, mass culture are perhaps all symptomatic of urbanisation, industrialisation and consumer culture. In the initial stages of industrial development, the emphasis is on production since the demand is great and the products are still scare. At the second stage it is the distribution network that has to be established. Now demand equals supply, but one has to be able to locate the sources of demand and then supply at those places. This second phase is key to understanding the concept of the proliferation of mass media.

Mass media consists of those mediums — radio, television, newspaper — which are meant to reach a large number of people. The emphasis is on quantity. In order to be able to reach the people with demand, it is necessary to reach a large number of people as effectively and as generally as possible. Once a product has reached the people and supply exceeds demand, the problem that confronts the producer is selling his goods. This brings one to the third phase where demand has to be *created* — where there is no desire, create desire. As in politics, here also, propaganda, untruth and lies come in a big way. But more important, quantity has now become still more significant. What goods (or services) are produced will depend upon the quantitative need for them.

In other words, man has to be reduced to a metonymic function. He is an unit of the total quantity + the desire for a certain good. In this situation he is a mere number and a mere part. Being a part of a large number he is *anonymous*. The totality of his identity is reducibe to whether he is majority or a minority in the mass.

The position reached thus is very similar to the position which we reached earlier through an analysis of the recent trends in language theories. This raises at least two significant questions.

1. Does this have anything to do with the language theory?
2. What role does language play in case of the mass man?

The answer to the first question is difficult. To say that the people are manipulated or influenced by mass media will be true. But to what extent is mass media influenced by intellectual theories? It is difficult to say. Perhaps, the language the mass media uses as well as the metalanguage of the present language theories evolve from the same historical process. To attempt to say any more would be beyond the scope of this paper.

The answer to the second question follows from the answer to the first. If we still believe that we communicate or miscommunicate through language, can be influenced, manipulated or provoked by language, then we cannot deny that mass media is capable of, is mainly used to fulfil these functions. It also brings us to the language of propaganda — a language to which the mass man is overexposed both as a political entity and as a consumer.

As a consumer, sponge or interpreter of this language, the mass man has very little space. So much of information, propaganda, temptation and lies are fed to him everyday that he can hardly separate one from the other. In this shortage of time, in a temporal asthma, he is mostly swayed by what happen around him, by what others do. Thus, the mass is, at critical periods, transformed into an unthinking mob.

Here, if one of the functions of language is to make one think, it is unsuccessful. On the other hand, what is the nature of this language, from where do the words come, who speaks them, who writes them, whose voice does one hear?

The questions themselves are muted against mass media. The flow of words is immense. But who wrote the article? Whose voice do I hear on the radio? Whose image is it that I find on the screen? Before I can register these facts, still more words, voices and images come my way. The mass man relies entirely on short-term memory. Books and songs go out of fashion each weekend. One is left only with scraps of passages and images without *history*. There is no time for history.

The Personal Crisis

This leads to a personal crisis. As the Buddha said, I live from moment to moment. But the difference is that this is not a position which I accept by choice. It is one which has been imposed upon me. Instead of pure perception I move towards pure chaos. I do not shed my identity willingly. My identity is ripped off me. I am the eternal atom. Around me relationships change. My house changes. My technology changes. I am a space without memory, an emptiness, where words combine and recombine, articulate themselves and again dissolve. Texts form, reform, deform. I am pure desire.

This would be all very good if man did not have an innate need for identity. However unstable, however uncertain, however flowing like water or like the flame of a lamp.[11] There is this innate urgent desperate *desire* for identity, for stability.

It is this which has to be acknowledged and respected. My essential humanness is in my attempt, however unsuccessful, of finding my relation with my world. And I do it essentially through language, through concepts.

---

11. *Questions of King Milinda*, Vol. I, Sacred Books of the East Series, Motilal Banarsidass, Delhi, 1998.

Man needs to have his personal history reffirmed. He needs to talk to other about who he is or who he thinks he is. For this, we not only need a language which still holds, however faintly, the possibility of a tentative stability, we also need enough time — for the act of internalising language means reaction with memory. And memory needs time. It is this aspect of language and languaging which needs rethinking.

Can I Really Touch You?

Let us now see if such rethinking is possible. Saussure told us that word/sound/chain of letters refer to a concept. In fact, the word, as we understand it, is made of a sound pattern, uttered or unuttered, and a corresponding concept. Together they make up a *sign*.

Sign = signifier (sound) + signified (concept)

In doing this we can no longer say that in language we talk about 'things' or can touch 'things'. The world of language, thus, becomes complete in itself. Taken further, we reach a position where there is no way out of the world of language into the world of things. The Buddhist theory of *apoha* also approaches everything, even identification, through negation. Selfhood is denied. But there still is something beyond the world, i.e., *nirvāṇa*. But today we are caught up in a world of meanings which are not stable, where we cannot refer to anything which is outside of language. Derrida begins his essay with a quote from Montaigne: "We need to interpret interpretations more than to interpret things."[12] He takes the position to its extreme. In fact, he asks if it is possible to talk about *things* in language. He points out that no discourse is capable of a determinate set of meaning. "(L)anguage bears within itself the necessity of its own critic."[13] Language, when seen thus, is capable of infinite interpretation, infinite *play*.

After the initial euphoria of the freedom has subsided, after the excitement of these new discoveries (sic) has waned, what confronts

12. Jacquies Derrida, "Structure, Sign and Play", *Modern Criticism*, p. 108.
13. *Ibid.*, p. 111.

us is the possibility of chaos. Language threatens to breakdown. Where there is no articulation there is uneasy silence, a silence which has come abruptly, without any preparation for it. In fact, Derrida himself is very much aware of this ominous possibility. He warns that we must not turn our eyes away

> ...when faced by the as yet unnameable which is proclaiming itself and which can do so . . . under the species of the nonspecies, in the formless, mute, infant and terrifying form of monstrosity.[14]

It is in fact the attempt to anticipate and counter such a position which (to say the least) threatens our sanctity, that one must attempt. This very attempt to restore the communicative function to language would be an attempt at reasserting our very humanness.

What I am trying to say is that before I make any attempt to speak about a thing, what I must do is explain what I mean by that particular expression. True, many modern theorists would argue that what I am doing is using more words. And each of these words can mean various things variously. By the very attempt to use language to communicate, I am paving the way for an infinity of references, for an infinite variety of understanding and responses. This argument has a certain justification. But if it is completely accepted, then certain circularities are encountered. One, this very argument is through words and hence its meaning or referentiality is bound to breakdown. Else it will be understood in an infinite number of ways. In other words, from this position *one cannot speak*. Two, if this stance is accepted, then language would lead to only confusion and chaos and hence cannot be considered language any more whose basic quality is a certain cultural commonality. Since we still can say that to a certain degree we understand one another and the very fact that we have been invited to write about this and are now here means that we still manage communication with some degree of success.

However, what this brings to our notice is the fact that our understanding of words or things is subjective. A word not only

---

14. Jacquies Derrida, "Structure, Sign and Play", *Modern Criticism*, p. 112.

refers to a number of things, it also has associations to a number of personal experiences. A word is not just what it means in the dictionary, in etymology, in time, it is also all that it means within my private space. It is a sponge for my memories. This is the word in its subjective colour. It is something which the other person does not know about, will never know unless I tell him.

True, language is an imperfect representation of reality. If the attempt to recreate reality through language is successful, what we shall have is another world — a successful cloning where, if history and time are removed, the order of cloning is reversible, there is no original, no copy. But given this nature of language and given the subjective consciousness of each man, what must be attempted is an adjustment. This adjustment must take into consideration certain facts and certain desires.

1. I want to reach, communicate, however incompletely, with another man.
2. In order to do so I must acknowledge him as an individual.
3. In acknowledging him as a man, I must also realise that he is subjective, and in many ways different from me.
4. If the communication is to be successful, I must make clear what I understand by a certain thing so that he can know how I am different from him, and *accept* my differences.
5. Finally, in spite of our differences we still wish to reach each other.

True, some theories including Derrida have looked positively at this free-play of meaning — "a world of signs without fault, without truth, without origin. . . ."[15] But such a metalanguage perpetually threatens neurosis. As I mentioned earlier, man has an innate and urgent desire for *stability*. True, it neither applies to his body and its metabolism nor to the language he uses. But it is within the tentative framework of stability he must proceed. If at all we can make the claim that we have made any advance in our understanding of language today, it is only at the threat of total breakdown of the

---

15. Jacquies Derrida, "Structure, Sign and Play", *Modern Criticism*.

system. If that happens, we will begin again (nobody knows from where) and complete another cycle.

The other approach, the more same approach, is to stop, if it is possible. One might immediately raise the objection that this is a subjective approach. The attempt that is now to be made is to understand language and man at the level of *parole* — specific instances of speech. My answer is emotional.

Did we not have enough of language system? Has it made things any easier for us? Whenever we try to understand even the language system, do we not approach it only through the specific use of language? The outcome of our understanding or *dis*-understanding — is it not articulated only through a specific use of language?

What Do I Mean by Humanism?

It is about this awareness of a word, a sentence, an encounter, a story or even a paper that I am talking. Communication is sharing. And sharing does not mean uttering or writing something which will float in someone else's memory like a bad solvent. It is also sharing a part of yourself, a part of your history so that the other person, beyond the language system or science of signs, becomes aware of you as a subject, as an entity. It is in this context that I talk of Humanism and understand Humanism. By Humanism I mean the attempt to acknowledge and then understand the other person's similarity with the difference from me. And next, it is an attempt to understand myself and the other's emotionality. He is neither a mere function in a signification system, nor a space where words are articulated and bonded to form discourses or texts.

In the Indian context today, language is significant in two ways. On the one hand, it is still possible to have a working definition of Humanism when we take our cultural context into account. On the other, and equally significant, we must use a language that can reach the common Indian and reach him with a certain poignancy and urgency.

Part II
Applications

Heidegger, Humanism and the Crisis of Applied Philosophies

Ravi Raj Singh

HEIDEGGER is one of those contemporary thinkers who have striven to expose the essential features of our age of technology. In his probes of the historical unfolding of the distinctive characteristics of our times he critically examines modern concepts and movements such as subject-ism, humanism, technology as well as the fundamental transformations in the character of religiosity, art and science. What we innocently characterise as the chief achievements of our age are stripped away by Heidegger to expose the profound spiritual losses in the midst of gains too often celebrated. In his post-*Being and Time* works Heidegger often outlines in his inimitable style and terminology the profound transformations that our times have brought forward. The forgetfulness of Being, the ever-deepening of subject-ism, and the collapse of metaphysics are recurrent themes in Heidegger's critiques he refuses to extol the virtues of technology and condone the destruction of the earth in the name of progress.

In our brief examination of Heidegger's unique exposition of modernity we will focus on his critique of humanism and the impact that humanistic presuppositions are having on what is expected from philosophy in our times. We will examine Heidegger's standpoints on issues such as the following: What does humanism stand for? Is philosophy being pressed into service of humanism? Is there such a thing as applied philosophy as opposed to theoretical philosophy? What is expected from philosophy in this age of technology? In order to understand Heidegger's position on these issues we have to not only consider his account of the culmination of the forgetfulness of Being in contemporary philosophy but also his extraordinary standpoints on modernity and humanism.

Heidegger analyses the implications of the deep-seated subjectism in the modern times in *Being and Time*[1] and several of his later works. He provides us with a comprehensive critique of humanism in his "Letter on Humanism"[2] (1947) and some remarks on anthropological tendencies of the modern age in his lecture-essay "The Age of the World Picture"[3] (1952). "Letter on Humanism" contains Heidegger's response to the French philosopher Jean Beaufret who had asked Heidegger a specific question, namely "How can one restore meaning to the word humanism?" Heidegger replies with the following comment:

> This question is asked with the intention of retaining the word 'humanism'. I wonder if it is necessary. Or is the harm wrought by all such terms not obvious enough yet?[4]

Heidegger repeats Beaufort's question a few pages later and remarks further:

> your question not only presupposes that you want to retain the word 'humanism' but it also contains the admission that the word has lost its meaning.[5]

Why is Heidegger so averse to humanism? Obviously no serious thinker ought to be opposed to the pursuit of human good or to a

---

1. Martin Heidegger, *Being and Time*, tr. by John Macquarie and Edward Robinson, New York: Harper and Row, 1962.
2. Martin Heidegger, "Letter on Humanism", tr. by Edgar Lohner in William Barrett and Henry D. Aiken (ed.), *Philosophy in the Twentieth Century*, Vol. 3, New York: Random House, 1962.
3. Martin Heidegger, "The Age of the World-Picture", tr. by William Lovitt in *The Question Concerning Technology and Other Essays*, New York: Harper and Row, 1977.
4. Heidegger, "Letter on Humanism", p. 272.
5. *Ibid.*, p. 290.

philosophical investigation concerning the status of human being in the scheme of things. Before explaining his objections to the contemporary movement of humanism, Heidegger traces some of its popular meanings and its history. It may be said that humanism is

> to reflect and to care that man be human and not . . . inhuman, i.e., outside of his essence. Yet, of what does the humanity of man consist? It rests in his essence. But whence and how is the essence of man determined?[6]

Heidegger refers to some classical interpretations of the essence of man. For Marx, social man is the natural man. The Christian views the humanity of man as the delimitation of *deitie*s, man as the child of God. The term *humanita*s first emerged and was earnestly pursued in the Roman times when *homo humanus* was deemed opposed to the *homo barbarus*. The Romans traced the human virtues through the incorporation of *paideia* as exposed by the Greeks. Historically speaking humanism has always coincided with attempts to revise the Greek world as evidenced in the eighteenth-century humanism of Winchelmann, Goethe and Schiller. However, humanism of Marx, as well as of Sartre, one that equates it with existentialism, do not and need not return to antiquity.

After having given this historical assessment, Heidegger expresses his objection to humanism as follows. No matter how different these kinds of humanism are,

> all of them coincide in that the *humanitas* of the *homo humanus* is determined from the view of an already established interpretation of nature, of history, of world, of the basis of the world (*Weltgrund*), i.e., of beings in their totality. Every humanism is either founded in a metaphysics or is converted into the basis for a metaphysics. Every determination of the essence of man that presupposes the interpretation of beings without asking the question of the truth of Being . . . is metaphysical.[7]

6. Heidegger, "Letter on Humanism", p. 275.
7. *Ibid*., p. 276.

Thus, according to Heidegger not only that humanism is metaphysical but all metaphysics is 'humanistic'. In establishing the humanity fails to take into account the relation between the essence of man and Being of beings. Beings metaphysically derived humanism 'neither knows nor understands' the role of Being and what Being has to do with the dignity of man. In rekindling the question of Being, Heidegger of course rejects the view of man as *animal rationale* which is but a convoluted metaphysical reinterpretation in the name of a translation of the Greek *zoon logon ehon*. In fully recognising the essence of man in man's relation with Being man is called *Dasein* or the being constituting the 'there' of Being. The essence of man is also called 'ex-sistence' by Heidegger which is not the same as the medieval term 'existentia', or even 'existence', which according to Sartre, precedes essence. "The essence of *Dasein* lies in its existence." This statement that appears in *Being and Time*[8] is explained as follows by Heidegger:

> man is essentially such that he is 'Here' (*Da*), i.e., within the clearing of Being. This Being of the Here, and only this, has the basic trait of ex-sistence, i.e., it stands outside itself within the truth of Being.[9]

In speaking of a 'clearing' and of 'ex-sistence' Heidegger labours to set aside the metaphysical bifurcation of reality into subjects and objects. The clearing is an arena in which there happens a setting-free of entities, in which an entity appears as itself, in which beingness of beings is rendered explicit. In the clearing, man's openness (ex-sistence) and appearance of entities come together. This cannot be described as a subject-object relation nor can this manifestation of entities be called 're-presentation'. According to Heidegger, this clearing or yielding of Being is not something that happens entirely due to man's projection toward entities, nor is it 'objective' in the sense of a permanent light of reason. This clearing is historically determined and itself subject to change in the passing of one era of the history of thought to another. Thus the clearing in which Aristotle stood is not the same as that in which Hegel

8. Heidegger, *Being and Time*, p. 42.
9. Heidegger, "Letter on Humanism", p. 278.

outlined his system. To inquire into the 'sendings' (*die Schicken*) of Being in different ages of philosophy is the task of 'thinking'. Metaphysics remains oblivious to such transformations within the clearing. It seeks and presupposes rather a permanent clearing and timeless truths concerning the subjectivity of the subject.

Thus, according to Heidegger, both historical and modern brands of humanism are based on metaphysically established interpretation "of nature, of history of world, of the basis of the world (*weltgrund*)".[10] In its affirmation of the status of man as the centre of reality, humanism nevertheless, fails to find the dignity of man in his relation with Being, for all metaphysical systems remain oblivious of the truth of Being. Man is an entity distinguished from all other entities by its connection with Being.

> Yet Being-what is Being? It is itself. Future thought must learn to experience and to express this. 'Being' is neither God nor the basis of the world. Being is further from all that is being and yet closer to man than every being, be it a rock, an animal, a work of art, a machine. . . . Man first clings always and only to beings. But when thought represents beings as beings it no doubt refers to Being.[11]

Modern humanism perpetuates this blindness toward the question of Being and at the same time, remains entrenched in metaphysical thinking and fails to define man in terms of his fundamental ontological capacity, namely that man's Being constitutes the 'Here' of Being, that Being needs and uses man in order that what-is may come to be. Thought has not yet learnt to experience and express 'what is Being'. Since our language is rooted in metaphysical structures, we lack the capacity and terminology to express the fundamental ontological status of man. Thinking, which is but thinking of Being must learn to hold on to initial and purer emergence before it disintegrates into customary and metaphysical interpretations. The thinker's thinking must overcome metaphysical philosophising in recognising and raising the question of Being.

---

10. Heidegger, "Letter on Humanism", p. 276.
11. *Ibid.*, p. 281.

Thus, we cannot fail to notice that the "Letter on Humanism" is not only a radical critique of the much acclaimed movement called 'humanism' but also an exposition, in Heidegger's own words, of his basic philosophical stance as well as an explication of the important terms coined and used by him in his previous works. One of the major preoccupations of the later Heidegger is to outline the basic features of modernity and especially of our age of technology. In the works that appear after the publication of *Being and Time*, he not only refers to the omissions in terms of a forgetfulness of Being in the works of the major Western philosophers, but also examines through acute historical assessments, important aspects of the contemporary human condition and the currently dominant world-view. In some of these works, while he composes a comprehensive critique of modernity, he also gives us his arguments concerning the nature and role of philosophy and responds to many of the current misconceptions of and mistaken expectations from philosophy and philosophers in this age of rapid social change and reckless applications of technology in the name of progress.

Individuals engaged in the field of philosophy today are showing the symptoms of a desire to play a significant role in the resolution of various human, social and cultural problems of the day. Not only that students and professors of philosophy are already embracing the ever-advancing but ever-sophisticating technologies for the purposes of research, teaching, and learning but some enthusiasts are in the business of modifying the very character and scope of philosophy. The introduction of applied philosophy and applied ethics courses, programmes and research and hiring of philosophers as resident ethicists in hospitals, corporations and government bodies may have enhanced the employment opportunities for professional philosophers. But is such a use of philosophy legitimate? Is the spirit of philosophy violated by such applications? Isn't the work of philosophers in the dangers of being indistinguishable from the day labours of the Journalists (lit. day-labourers). Would the Socratic gadfly be converted into "the paid wage labourers of the status quo?"[12]

---

12. James O. Young, "The Immorality of Applied Ethics", *The International Journal of Applied Philosophy*, 3 (1986), p. 40.

As part of his commentary on modernity, Heidegger has often warned his readers against the mistaken view of the role of philosophy in our times as well as about the sweeping impacts of the current applications of technology. At the same time, he is very much interested in the beginnings and the fundamentals of Western philosophy. Of course, as we conclude from the above sketch of the "Letter on Humanism", a philosophy is as far removed from 'thinking' as it can be if it does not raise the all important question concerning Being. One of the lucid reflections on the nature of philosophical questioning appears in Heidegger's *An Introduction to Metaphysics*:

> All essential philosophical questioning is necessarily untimely. This is so because philosophy is always projected far in advance of its time, or because it connects the present with its antecedent with what 'initially' was. Philosophy always remains a knowledge which not only cannot be adjusted to a given epoch but on the contrary imposes its measure upon its epoch.
>
> Philosophy is essentially untimely because it is one of those few things that can never find an immediate echo in the present, when such an echo seems to occur, when a philosophy becomes fashionable, either it is no real philosophy or it has been misinterpreted and misused for ephemeral and an extraneous purposes.
>
> Accordingly philosophy cannot be directly learned like manual and technical skills; it cannot be directly applied or judged by its usefulness in the manner of economic or professional knowledge.[13]

According to Heidegger, essential philosophical questioning is necessarily untimely, not because philosophy preoccupies itself with timeless verities, but because man's openness and the appearance of entities is historically determined. One cannot fathom the current yieldings and interpretations of Being, unless an historical assessment is made of previously evolved concepts/

---

13. Martin Heidegger, *An Introduction to Metaphysics*, tr. by Ralph Manheim, New Haven: Yale University Press, 1959, p. 8.

interpretations of Being. Thus, philosophy 'connects the present with its antecedent', i.e., philosophy cannot be a-historical and/or concerned exclusively with the current affairs. When a philosophy seems to be directly and immediately applicable to the present realities, it does not remain genuine philosophy; it is being misused. Heidegger strongly affirms that philosophy is not a skill that can be learned, applied and judged for its usefulness like other professional skills. The usefulness of philosophy cannot be measured by the same "everyday standards by which we judge bicycles and sulpher baths".[14] One may ask: why is the task of philosophy so ambiguously and so variously described by different philosophers. Heidegger responds as follows:

> There is no way of determining once and for all what the task of philosophy is, and accordingly what must be expected of it. Every stage and every beginning of its development bears within it its own law. All that can be said is what philosophy cannot be and cannot accomplish.[15]

Since every stage of philosophy 'bears within its own law', and since the essential concepts of every epoch have historically evolved but subject to change, the task and possibilities of philosophy cannot be defined once and for all. Since the reflections on the meanings of Being have to do with fundamentals and not specific cultural issues, our expectations from philosophy, must remain confined to basic, general, and historical considerations. Although the task of philosophy must remain ambiguous, nevertheless what philosophy cannot accomplish and ought not try to accomplish is clear enough: philosophy cannot meddle with specific cultural issues and/or propose swift resolutions of social problems. In some quarters,

> Philosophy is expected to promote and even to accelerate — to make easier as it were — the practical and technical business of culture. But — it is in the very nature of philosophy never to make things easier but only more difficult. And this is not merely because its language

---

14. Heidegger, *An Introduction to Metaphysics*, p. 12.
15. *Ibid.*, p. 9.

> strikes the everyday understanding as strange if not insane. Rather, it is the authentic function of philosophy to challenge historical Being-there and hence in the last analysis Being, pure and simple. It restores to things, to the entities their weight (Being).[16]

It is quite clear from the above that according to Heidegger, the beast called 'applied philosophy' does not exist. To make the so-called practical and technical business easier is no business of philosophy. The nature of philosophy is such that it does not make things easier but more difficult, that is, it reveals how problematic and complex things are, things that are dismissed as self-evident in our everyday, unphilosophical attitude. By referring to the issues of man's historical Being-there and by referring ultimately to Being as such, philosophy extends the problems at hand to the level of fundamental ontology. This cannot be called a mere explanation or clarification that would make things easier but rather by restoring the ontological to the ontic, that is, by restoring the extraordinary to the ordinary, philosophy, by no means, can subserve the cause of our (technological) times, but necessarily and essentially, must challenge and critically (and historically) evaluate the spirit of the times. Philosophy does not merely clarify and resolve current cultural problems; it does not make things lighter, easier and convenient, but it ends up making things heavier, the problems weightier by raising the question concerning Being.

> It is absolutely correct and proper to say that "you can't do anything with philosophy". It is only wrong to suppose that this is the last word on philosophy. For the rejoinder imposes itself: granted that we cannot do anything with philosophy, might not philosophy, if we concern ourselves with it, do something "with us"?[17]

Heidegger seems to say that philosophy changes things for us totally or not at all. It lifts us right out of our times so that we may gain the historical perspective on the emergence of the basic ideas of our age. A philosopher ought not waste his or her energies on

16. Heidegger, *An Introduction to Metaphysics*, p. 11.
17. *Ibid.*, p. 12.

unravelling the merits and demerits of a particular technology but must concentrate on the meaning and history of technology as such. A philosopher should not spend time on how to make the capitalist practice of advertising more ethical but must focus on issues such as the *raison d'être* of advertising as such or capitalism as such. Philosophy propels our thinking toward the fundamentals, exposed according to Heidegger, through the raising of the question of Being. Thus, he concludes in his lecture-essay "what is philosophy": "The expressly adopted and unfolding correspondence which corresponds to the appeal of the Being of what-is philosophy."[18] Philosophy is the historically unfolding co-respondence to Being which must shy away from assumed permanent verities of reason, rigid and a-temporal conceptualisations of metaphysics.

But the desire to create applied philosophies by down grading the original task of philosophy, not having the patience to let philosophy 'do something with us', or desiring to do things with philosophy, must amount to a transformation of the philosopher from a cultivator of philosophy to a master of philosophy. This tendency to press philosophy into the service of 'human' ends, is part and parcel humanism. As Heidegger remarks in his lecture-essay "The Age of the World Picture":

> The inter-weaving of these two events, which for the modern age decisive — that the world is transformed into picture and man into *subjectum* — throws light at the same time on the grounding event of modern History . . . namely, the more extensively and the more effectually the world stands at man's disposal as conquered, and the more objectively the object appears, all the more subjectively, i.e., the more importunately, does the *subjectum* rise up, and all the more impetuously, too, do observation of and teaching about the world change into a doctrine of man, into anthropology. It is no wonder that humanism first arises where the world becomes picture. It would have been . . . impossible for a humanism to have gained currency in

18. Martin Heidegger, *What is Philosophy*, tr. by W. Kluback and J.T. Wilde, New Haven: College and University Press, 1958, p. 91.

> the great age of the Greeks. Humanism, therefore in the more strict, historiographical sense, is nothing but a moral-aesthetic anthropology. The name 'anthropology' . . . designates that philosophical interpretation of man which explains and evaluates whatever is, in its entirety, from the standpoint of man and in relation to man.[19]

Thus, according to Heidegger, humanism is a byproduct of the historically arrived grand objectification of the world (i.e., the world having become picture-like) coupled with man having become the fundamental *subjectum*. This way of thinking has altered "the observation of and teaching about the world into a doctrine of man". As we have considered, the processes of humanism also affect the expectations that some scholars have from philosophy. The uses of philosophy are being increasingly defined from the standpoint of man. Heidegger reminds us that philosophy cannot afford to jeopardise its status as the most general science in the name of specific applications. Philosophy cannot be otherwise than the inquiry into Being.

---

19. Heidegger, "The Age of the World-Picture", p. 133.

Tyranny in Disguise
Expert Knowledge and Human Interest

Mahasweta Chaudhury

THE anxiety that scientific/expert knowledge has reached such a height in specialisation that individual freedom and ordinary reason are at stake is a genuine concern. In different areas of knowledge and life science and its practitioners enjoy a cognitively high status at the cost of other traditions. It is felt by many that this unquestionable authority of scientific knowledge over other practices can be challenged and other practices placed in the right context. Some thinkers also hold that ordinary reason (if not better) should be treated with the same kind of respect as scientific reason.

The high status conferred on science through many historical events resulted into role as a neutral arbiter of true and the rational. And this sacrosanct authority empowered science and the practitioners of science to the extent of tyranny.

This concern is genuine and it is to a great extent true that scientific knowledge has often played a tyrannical role both cognitively (disregarding other alternative traditions) and empirically. For these reasons scientific knowledge to many has become a suspect. Granting all these to the ciritics, we must at least distinguish between what science aims for and what actually it has achieved. Even granting that the tremendous power of scientific achievements have been exploited for political reasons and not so much for alleviation of human suffering, one may say that all these could only establish gross misuse of science and not that the latter is an irrational tyrannical institution. I argue that 'scientific' stands for a stance that is based on logic and reason compared to any other standpoint where other considerations may prevail, although it is arbitrary to mark modern science only as science and all other traditions as 'unscientific' or 'prescientific'.

We should emphasise in this connection that the allegeed tyrannical element lies not in the intrinsic nature of scientific knowledge but rather in its misuse or abuse by political power. However the general resentment is justifiable that most of the time people do not have enough information about achievements and decisions. More transparency about scientific activities and other details (such as expenses, time and the risks involved) is desirable in a free society. The example of jury system (a favourite example of Feyerabend infavour of ordinary reason) can show that the intuition and reasoning capacity of ordinary people should not be underestimated. In complicated legal processes jury system works quite statisfactorily.

But this argument is not applicable to scientific knowledge and dicisions in the same way. For the latter involves lot of background knowledge with technical details. The actual research processes are tedious, repetitive, perseverant routine activities of trial and error. It involves long equations, complex calculations, etc., which are not only uninteresting but also unintelligible to one outside the specialised circuit, let alone the ordinary people. Only the end-result, if successful, in any mundane way can interest outsiders. A space research scientist in the mid-sixties when asked about his research project answered that "without the tedious details, if it is successful, then people from every part of India can watch the same television programme". Surely we realise today that his project has been successful.

Another way we can understand the situation is by distinguishing between scientism and scientific knowledge, expertise and expert knowledge. Scientism is 'aping of science' as Hayek calls it — that is unnecessary stretching of science, a caricature of science. Expertise similarly is a particular skill in a particular area whereas expert knowledge ideally is a specialised knowledge that can interconnect (and sometime solve) a problem with many other interrelated areas. It is desirable indeed that expert knowledge should be explained in terms which are easily understandable by anyone. Otherwise a decision would appear to be unilateral and tyrannical due to lack of transparency. Medical or ecological cases particularly are in need of such dissemination of scientific knowledge.

One quite significant point is to be considered which works from within the scientific tradition. The objectivity claim of science is rejected from within by the indeterminacy principle. No tyrannical institution will specify the conditions under which it has to be rejected. But there are methodological devices such as placebo, double blind tests, instrumentation, etc., which act as safety guards from within the scientific tradition. It is similar to the blind referring system for publishing to check editorial tyranny. This is not to say that the actual practice is never tyrannical but only to argue that an institution as such cannot be termed tyrannical if it also includes methods to inhibit or at least minimise possibility of tyrannical treatment.

The problems related to domineering role of science and technology cannot be overestimated. Feyerabend's fiery diatribe against science has many substantive points. It is true that it is time one should be aware that Western tradition is engulfing all other traditions. Even concepts and language are entrenched by it. Why, for example, Western (mainly Anglo-American) culture is 'mainstream' and other cultures are 'alternative' cultures? Surely Eastern civilisation has at least some claim to be temporally prior. The division into 'First world'—'Third world' countries, 'developing' (a patronising change from 'underdeveloped') and 'developed' also is arbitrary and questionable. Feyerabend and many others are also right that Western science has been exploited more for accumulation of power than any human cause. Two areas can be particularly identified where individual rights are not respected. These two are medical profession and education where patients and students are exploited because transparency and accountability are lacking. It is not clear how to determine the sources of a physical/mental or intellectual treatment.

Granting all this to one who challenges this paternalistic picture, it is not clear that picture can be reversed without violating the basic tenets of freedom. I have discussed eleswhere[1] that Mannheim's 'militant democracy' to monitor all scientific dicisions

1. In my forthcoming book "Facets of Freedom" to be published by Indian Institute of Advanced Study, Shimla.

cannot be a viable democratic norm. Similarly, Feyerabend's slogan, 'Laymen can and must supervise Science' is not tenable either.[2] He thinks that "the errors of specialists can be discovered by ordinary people" only if they are prepared to do some hard work. There should be 'duly elected committees' to examine the safety of nuclear reactors or whether "scientific medicine deserves the unique position of theoretical authority". He thinks that scientists, educators, physicians must be supervised not only when engaged in *public* jobs; but must also be watched most carefully when called upon to solve the *problems* of an individual or a family in somewhat similar way as we watch plumbers and carpenters after comparing estimates from different firms.

It is undeniable that there is a patronising element in the way in which specialists treat lay person. But supervision or 'watching carefully' cannot solve the difficulty. Apart from the practical problem of understanding the technicalities in which plumbers and carpenters also excel in deluding laymen, there is some internal flaw in Feyerabend's argument. When he says 'duly elected committee of laymen' or 'people prepared to do some hard work' are qualified enough to do the 'supervision' of specialists, there is a tacit distinction made between other laymen and these 'duly qualified ones' which amounts to saying that the latter category is specialised to supervise. So we come back to the notion of specialist again only in the sense of a kind of super-specialist to watch ordinary specialists. Secondly, if ideology creeps into scientist's theory because they are human, these 'supervisors' are equally vulnerable to similar prejudices, more so because they are aware of their 'policing' role. Scientists at least face many checks internal to the system, but layman-supervisor have only poilitical ideology and therefore more chance of being prejudiced.

Besides these difficulties there is another more serious problem I see in such supervision to protect individuals from tyranny. My objection is that it is self-defeating. The practical problems aside, such project defeats the very cause it aims for. The basic point here is: expert scientific knowledge has in actual practice been often tyrannical. Now supervision is suggested as a way to watch if there

2. P. Feyerabend, *Science in a Free Society*, p. 96.

is any infringement of individual freedom. But scientists are also *free* individuals and their enterprise should be a *free* enterprise at least in a free society. No cognitive projects, especially scientific research, can be freely pursued if there is constant supervision or at least 'careful watching'. It will not only be a loss to progress of knowledge (no one can work or achieve successfully if there is someone breathing over his shoulder) but also infringement of individual freedom. It is a grave infringement since the area is particularly important for its creative and cognitive value.

Therefore supervision or monitoring cannot be viable methods to combat tyranny if there is any. It should be dealt with from within the tradition by methodological devices and transparency. Any such attempts from outside the tradition will only lead to more serious troubles including violation of freedom thus defeating the very aim these are aimed for. It is clear that the image of scientific research as a course of unilinear progressive nature is oversimplistic. Growth of scientific knowledge is neither steady nor monolithic. It can grow in diverse directions, stall sometimes and even include periodic phases. Human interests and social factors also can influence its direction and priorities. It would be a myopic methodology if other traditions are ignored and human factors overlooked. Instead of either having an attitude of reverence and complete trust on scientific experts or on the other hand undermining their positive achievements, a comprehensive appraisal of the issue of science and other traditions should be undertaken.

First, we should examine if attention and focus of scientific research is proportionate and reasonable from humanistic standpoint. Second, the more controversial area of research is that which concerns human problems directly (medical treatment, nutrition, birth control, genetic engineering, etc.) rather than areas remote from human concerns such as space research, nuclear science, geological and astronomical sciences. Finally, the battle between scientific and other traditions or the expert-laypeople controversies do not lead us anywhere. Instead of scientific expertise *vs.* other culture, we can say scientific expertise *and* other cultures in a cooperative sense. That kind of concept is not absolutely unknown—it is already embedded in our notion of interdisciplinary studies and enterprises.

Focus of Scientific Research

The most prevalent reason for resentment about scientific research tradition is that it allows disproportionate amount of attention and research funding to areas less vital or major problem area for most. Some problems that affect comparatively few people (e.g., infertility) receive more attention than problems that seems to be global in comparison. AIDS, famine in some countries, drought or flood conditions, etc., continue to 'simmer on the scientific back burner'. Indeed some attention and fund have been spared on these problems to certain extent but that did not help much. So a totally new approach is needed that requires a breakthrough from the traditional disciplinary barriers. It appears that enough attention (and therefore funding and time) is not given to many global problems concerning human welfare comparable to the enormous amount of research, time and money spent on other so-called prestige areas such as space research, superconductor, sophisticated armaments and defence equipments. One single example can indicate how a very major human affliction is neglected with sheer indifference by scientific community. The case I refer to is the case of malaria. Half a billion people catch malaria every year. There are other mosquito-borne diseases also (dengue, filaria, etc.) which claim thousands of lives every year. Quinine, the traditional medicine to cure malaria, still remains to be expensive to harvest, synthesise and yet fails to prevent relapses. Attempts by the World Health Organisation to eradicate the disease by killing the courier failed when anopheles mosquito became resistant to pesticide such as DDT. Almost half of the world's population is still vulnerable to this disease and desperately in need of a cheap and effective vaccine. But modern drug firms seem to ignore the need and lack motivation for related research efforts.

Western companies manufacture number of preventive medicine for rich tourists to malarial climes. Chloroquine for example provides (in combination with some other drugs) almost 70 per cent protection against the malarial parasite plasmodium. In higher dose it is also effective in curing patients who have malaria. But these drugs are far too expensive for those most at risk, 90 per cent of malarial victims being sub-Saharan Africans and moreover plasmodium is fast becoming resistant to them. Mefloquine is a stronger prophylactic than Chloroquine and is effective in 90 per cent cases but it is even more expensive and has side effects (a British Medical Journal study reports that one in 140 users suffer incapacitating dizziness, panic attacks, hallucinations or other neuropsychiatric problems.

Given the enormity of the malaria menace (half a billion catching it of whom 2 million dying every year), it seems that malaria research should attract more attention. But the world spent less to research on the killer protozoa than even on asthma and AIDS. It seems governmental research agencies show more effort than private pharmaceutical companies. The real reason behind the apathy is commercial — most of the victims are too poor to pay for the medicine being from Asian and African countries. And if the tourist market is the target, the risks are high because in that case the use is preventive only for the well-to-do customers from developed countries. In case of any failure or adverse effects they can bring litigation against the companies. But this neglect in the focus of research on malaria is short-sighted because with the steady changes in world climate, malaria can also come back to Western countries from which the killer disease left a century ago.

More Controversies in Human Areas than in Non-Human Problem Areas

It has already been pointed out that problem areas that directly or indirectly affect human beings are not the priority areas of research and they are also subject to controversy. Space research, geological and astronomical sciences involve programmes whose main target is more knowledge about these areas, not solving some human problems. The latter may be a secondary consequence but improving human conditions is not the principal aim of these scientific research programmes. There may be some minor points of difference among rival paradigms in those sciences but not so much debates and disagreements as found in areas that concern human welfare to some extent. The reason behind the disagreements is that between the two goals of sciences, namely knowledge of nature and solution of human problems, there is usually no debate about the first as such. But when the second is also taken into account, there is a number of questions that can be raised. Should we search for knowledge's sake only or should all-scientific research aim at human good? Is it possible to set some moral goals for scientific pursuits or should scientists be given complete freedom to pursue knowledge? And so on. The notion of science policy therefore, becomes very significant. But again if science policy is decided by some super, extra-scientific norm, there is always a risk of either paternalism or guidance by some ideology. Both are threats to scientific freedom. So when human problems and their minimisation (if not solution) are concerned, it is difficult to decide whether scientists should work in absolute freedom in search of 'truth' especially because of time and fund constraints. Even a naïve layman is justified in thinking why can't scientific knowledge control devastating floods, epidemics and other calamities whereas enormous amount of money and human resources are being spent on knowing the nature of celestial bodies, palaeolithic age or intricacies of microbodies and son on?

Scientific Expertise and Non-Scientific Traditions

The debate whether science is the most prestigious (if not the only) cognitive programme or merely one of many traditions has become a bitter issue and a defunct cliche. Indeed science as a research tradition has belied many of our hopes and aspirations. The general frustration is so enormous that now people are gradually turning to other traditions for their comfort. Instead of only condemning this phenomenon as regressive and superstitious, one should make an in-depth analysis of why anti-scientific or pre-scientific traditions are slowly gaining ground in many countries.

Prayer, Faith healing, Reiki and Pranic (the last two being Asian modes of healing by touch) systems of cure of many ailments are steadily getting popular even in Western countries. The most astonishing turn is that some scientists are beginning to look seriously at just what benefits patients (say after a open-heart surgery) may derive from extra-scientific practices like prayer or touch and so on.[3] It is held by many that as the twentieth century draws to an end,

---

3. "Healing", Claudia Wallis, *Time*, 24 June 1996 gives a well documented accounted of how in America not only people are turning to extra-scientific modes of healing but the scientists →

> there is growing disenchantment with one of its greatest achievements: modern high-tech medicine. Western medicine is at its best in crisis-battling infection, repairing the wounds of war, replacing a broken-down kidney or heart.[4]

But increasingly what ails people of modern societies are chronic illnesses such as high blood pressure, bodyaches, arthritis, cardiovascular disease, depression, even cancer and AIDS all of which are stress and lifestyle related diseases. These are not merely bodily problems, therefore other traditional practices that take the mind also into account can give relief and solace to a great extent in these cases. The effects of religion, prayer and touch, etc., on healing are of course debatable except the psychological element. The traditional medical systems (*Āyurveda*, Yunani, Homeopathy, etc.) are however *not* based on spirituality and therefore are of testable nature. More research on these practices can be useful in the sense that their claim to knowledge can only be legitimised if the dominant scientific tradition sanctions their methods. One way to such recognition is through their inclusion in the main stream educational curriculum. With such idea in mind Ashis Nandy[5] says that universities in India

> have to develop a new openness to and protectiveness towards non-modern, local systems of knowledge. These systems are the ones which need protection now, not the modern ones.

→also are researching seriouly for the effect or religion and faith-related practices on patients. "Twenty years ago, no self-respecting American doctor would have dared to propose a double-blind, controlled study of something as intangible as prayer. Western medicine has spent the past 100 years trying to rid itself of remnants of mysticism. . . . Today . . . a shift among the doctors in the US toward the view that there may be more to health than blood-cell counts and EKGs and more to healing than pills and scalpels."

4. *Ibid.*, p. 39.
5. Ashis Nandy, "The Future University", *Seminar*, January 1995, p. 96.

He envisages the role of future universities not serving

> only as repositories of knowledge valued in the famous Western centres of scholarship but they have to inculcate a robust suspicion towards the victorious systems of knowledge, and stress the recovery and transmission of knowledge that has been cornered or defeated.

Nandy made three propositions:

(1) Recovery of indigenous knowledge is not easy because modern (scientific) knowledge is available in a 'readymade capsuled form'. The damage caused by mindless consumerism can be repaired by the university.

(2) The dialogue between the traditional and the modern has broken down. The university can mediate between the dialogue of vernacular knowledge acquired over the centuries and the more elegantly packaged, laboratory-based knowledge.

(3) The job of a centre for higher learning is not to produce a perfect human being but rather for making possible a range of options for people and society to freely choose from.

No one can agree more with Nandy on these points particularly the third proposition. Indeed the aim of higher learning is to create an ambience of freedom and rationality. No goodwill come out of any kind of social engineering. His vision of future university as a mediator between tradition and modern forms of knowledge sounds reasonable particularly if we consider how much area of our modern life is taken out of traditional participatory style and given to experts. In traditional India most of the areas (even medical treatment) were shared by the people of the community with some degree of specialisation. Now experts reign in every areas, even bridal make-up, wedding managements are in the hands of experts. Therefore, staying outside the modern system of knowledge would only give tradition the status of an 'alternative system'. To be effective, it is prudent to be part of the mainstream modern institution such as university which is regarded as the mainstay of the expertise of different sort.

To conclude it is not clear that scientific expertise is not to be found in the specialised skills of its practitioner or that specialisation and its associated expertise is "simply a strategy for being a player in the epistemic marketplace".[6] Fuller's main contention is that rhetorical strategies used by scientists are responsible for people's trust in their expertise. The recurrent theme of his work is that the optimal way to democratise science is to detach it from any specialised status and practice. This theme is not very different from the Feyerabendian position. Democratic practice also is the common key notion. Knowledge production should be encouraged with maximal public involvement, open to all people, irrespective of their expertise and often despite their lack of scientific training. It is true that specialists take a narrow view of problems and do not relate it to larger projects. So the question still remains that competence of scientific expertise is not uncontestable at least in the public sphere of global problems. But it is not clear that scientific expertise has nothing to offer in the solution of these problems. Specialised knowledge has an important role to play (say in curbing an epidemic or AIDS as an immunological problem) here as well. But what is lacking in this approach is the lack of co-ordinated effort from other disciplines as well to have a comprehensive approach to the problem. Universities so far freed only experts without this vision. In Nandy's view perhaps this lack of coordination is indicated. Thus, the best way to supplement expert knowledge is not democratisation of science by lay-people (which involves further problems as discussed before) but interdisciplinary participation that helps realignment of scientific talent and other expert knowledge to a common concern. Indeed sociologists, historians, geographers, anthropologists and most importantly philosophers can supplement expert knowledge for a better understanding of problems in a global perspective. This idea is already implicit in the concept of science policy which however needs to be redefined and refurbished from time to time.

---

6. Kuhn, Feyerabend and most sociologists of knowledge are of such opinion. Recently Steve Fuller suggested that rhetorical strategies have effectively removed scientific decision-making from public scrutiny. See his *Philosophy, Rhetoric and the End of Knowledge*, 1993.

Humanism in a Developing Society
From Two Cheers to Three Cheers?

Vinay Hardikar

The world is too much with us; late and soon
Getting and spending, we lay waste our powers
Little we see in Nature that is ours:
We have given our hearts away, a sordid boon!

— William Wordsworth

WHEN Wordsworth made the above observations about two hundred years ago, he could not have been referring to, by even the widest and wildest guess, the topic of this short paper. Nevertheless it is equally difficult to imagine that Wordsworth did not imply, particularly in the third line, something of irrevocable relevance to this paper and also the entire three-day-exercise we have undertaken. The very phrase, 'Nature that is ours', is loaded enough to start ringing an orchestra of bells of various sizes, tenors and volumes. Further, the phrase enriches possible implications by its ambiguity over 'our nature' and what 'Nature wished us to do' — the most likely poles for any discussion of humanism; and the pointed sarcasm of the last line — the sordid boon that befalls those who have been reckless enough to give their hearts away — should serve as a statutory warning for all times.

Though methodologically imperative, it is futile, one feels, to look for exact meaning of the term 'Humanism' in new or old dictionaries; as the dictionaries fail to place it in the context a seminar like the present one underlines. Dictionaries describe humanism in two ways — firstly, and perhaps rather oddly from our viewpoint, as the renaissance revival of studies of classical literature and then, in the modern age, as a philosophy wherein man is the measure of all things with particular stress on human values, man's superiority to Nature and the free will of man. But when we venture to talk of humanism in the post-cold war ethos we find ourselves entrapped in, we imply many more things. Secularism, democracy, rule of law, gender equality, freedom from want, to name but a few. We also hint at a basic 'humane' approach to other beings which are as much a part of Nature as we are. Moreover we also presuppose a civic society and a political system which will ensure the enjoyment of the above attributes by, ideally all, but practically most members of such a society — in other words humanism ceases to be an abstraction and attracts all sorts of real life situational connotations. In still different words, humanism can be said to imply rectification of whatever shortcomings we may observe in the current way of life.

Indeed, humanism should come first as an ideology for any community and it should never take the back seat in an undeveloped society. But history seems to be fond of, like the wanton boy in *King Lear*, treating the have-nots of the world to black humour by first misleading them to various other 'isms' which promise to rid mankind of all or most ills that are unmatched in their dogged adherence to it, and after the have-nots had enough of the various isms — which are in essence reconstructions and conjectures, inspiredly or meticulously worked out by gods (supposedly), god-men, seers and philosophers, rationalists and scientists analysts of history, economists and political leaders — a lot, it would be wrong to suppose, were hampered by poor intelligence or scholarship, they turn to humanism. The potential of these isms to invade and distort mankind's perception of itself is, history will testify, immense. Isms are brilliant because they highlight only certain aspects of the human predicament and blur our vision of ourselves enticing us to accept total solutions which are really based on partial and at times one-sided analyses. Man is the proud creation of Nature and enjoys the special gift in that man can observe, understand, decipher the innumerable processes and some of the secrets of Nature. But how and why men fell short of understanding one another, developed notions of superiority and inferiority gave rise to a hierarchical idea of society and discovered the pleasures of power over fellow human being? Running into various kinds of puzzlement over the awe-inspiring positive and negative exhibitions of what Nature was capable of, when did man decide that it was better to take recourse to the supernatural, invent God and go after that creation of his own imagination as an individual pursuit and develop a feeling of moral superiority over other human beings? Why did mankind consistently fail to inspire the mutual confidence that issues of this existence could be resolved better by creating ways of 'man to man' and not by justifying 'the ways of God to Man?' Why is it that — though rich in poetic vision and promising in philosophical content the holy scriptures of all religions start dragging their feet when it comes to the establishment and governance of a civil soicety? Why is it that the most religious and the most god-fearing people generally throw up the most backward and the most fragmented social structure and the neighbour (*sic*. Neighbouring country) is more often hated that loved?

The admixture of good and evil, of human and inhuman of refined and bestial which is encountered in most conventionally religious societies is generally wrongly blamed on human nature and is seldom regarded as a natural fallout of the essentially irrational manner religions adopt towards human existence by placing faith ahead of reason. Religions also presuppose the existence of agents of good and evil beyond the control of human intelligence and perception and order humans to cultivate good and reject evil without ever clearly defining what is good and what is evil in situations close to everyday life. Maxims like all men are children of God and there is an element of the Divine in not only all humans but also animals may hold, if they hold at all, only in abstract philosophical context but would prove hollow for modern governance and relations of one society (*sic*. country) to another. Same goes for the maxim that no religion teaches or encourages indifference or hatred of other religions — the history of mankind being replete with wars fought between followers of different religions as well as wars between follower of different sects within one religion. In ancient times most religions did throw up social systems like the *cāturvarṇya* or the *śariat* which, it is needles to say, imply more harm than good in the modern context. Religions form one of the unsurmountable hurdles in the march towards a humanistic approach because they have never been able to keep pace with the dynamism of man in unsolving the phenomenon of the physical world and applying that knowledge towards attainment of a better life in this world.

Ironical as it may appear the term humanism did attract its broadly comprehensive modern connotations only after and due to the post-renaissance advances in science which, on the one hand, led to a systematic understanding of nature and on the other hand encouraged basic exploration of this world. Though the concepts of world and universe did exist before the renaissance, their implications were narrow in the geographical sense and most of the times controlled by the particular religion the user belonged to. Post-renaissance spirit of inquiry not only started a spate of discoveries and inventions in natural sciences but also resulted in the birth of social sciences in the primary form with rudiments of economics, political science and sociology all clubbed together. At this juncture, it should have been but natural for humanism to have won over acceptance over traditional religion-dominated philosophy, ethics and systems of governance. It should be called one of the most unfortunate coincidences of history, one feels, the modern scientific progress was attributed to nations the scientists belonged to and the kings who ruled those nations most of the times *in tandem* with the religious authority. A king may have encouraged research and exploration but his rule was sanctified not by the rich promise those advances held for mankind as a whole but only by religious authority which generally had little or no interest in matters of this world and was busy with self-aggrandisement and the clout over gullible populations of still feudal masses. This unplanned sabotage of the march towards humanism was more damaging to mankind than many a man-hatched and executed conspiracy. The medieval nationalism were centred on rules as persons or houses of rulers and prevented the acceptance of a world-view which aimed at better and more refined life for all citizens of the nation and the modern nationalisms remained territory and tradition centred to negate once again attitudes which would deal with problems of mankind as a whole.

The record of post-renaissance ideologies and isms is no better. Capitalism reeked of exploitation and, in the words of Dickens, 'murdered the innocents'. Communism, the scientific antithesis of Capitalism, murdered one and all and turned individuals against themselves in the name of purgation — thus violating the basic dignity of the individual to be what he is. Colonialism divided the mother earth into vast tracts of servitude and those who benefited from that. Socialism created the monster of bureaucracy wherever it was practised and its German face, 'national socialism' led to the holocaust — one of the most shameful and inhuman memories of post-Renaissance, post-Enlightenment history. Despite the best efforts of the United Nations, in times of peace preparations for war never ceased and some lobbies would go out of business if countries did not fight one another. Worse still, if a country is reluctant to fight another country, dissent, secession and infighting can be engineered through across the border terrorism to set one section of its people against another. Innocents can be wiped out in the name of justice democracies increasingly tend to become oligarchical and later tyrannical or get bogged down because of corrupt governmental and/or scandalous leaders.

As if these ideologies had not played enough havoc with the advancement of mankind individualism cotinuously raises its proud head time and again. Obscurantist as the traditional philosophies and religions might have been their share of individualism mercifully was manifest only in spiritual pursuits; only the seers and seekers of the Divine exemplified individualism in extreme form. But the pursuit of happiness which the modern era sanctioned as one of the basic rights of the individual (as a member of a collective, one would like to stress) tends to throw up forms of individualism which object to the basic tenets of humanism inasmuch as they place the inclination of one individual ahead of those of his fellow beings. The fundamental truth that freedom and self-realisation can be meaningful and elegant only when exercised in the company of others is totally lost sight of. Professionalism and globalism are two more watchwords to have emerged in the last quarter of this century which have further compounded the debate over the possibe emergence of a humanistic way to things because professionalism tends to depend on the principle of success being self-justified and globalism is yet to free itself of the hangover of colonialism, materialism and the artificial division of the globe during the cold war and its aftermath ceulur. If the humanistic approach was sabotaged by nationalism in the eighteenth and nineteenth centuries, it is being torpedoed by individualism and suspect globalism in the twentieth century. The same is true for the very recent guiding principle of 'perform or perish' in the New Economic Order which totally ignores the consideration of why some parts of the world cannot perform on par with some others. The developed and developing nations are not so because their people chose to be such but precisely because during the anomalous history we inherit some nations progressed and prospered at the expense of others. How can we expect a fair competition between them unless there is unanimity that even competition will have a humane face?

The regular invasions of mankind's perception of itself and the consequent distortions of perspective created the world of imbalances we discuss endlessly and also to no end. One is almost tempted to conclude that mankind has been passing from one anomalous situation to another and we are probably running frantically to remain in the same place. While the achievements in the fields of science, technology, communication, medicine and defence are staggering; art, literature and culture have shown significant advances, one wonders whether the basic nature of man has undergone any subtle change, and, if it has, whether the change has been for the better or the worse. Moreover, these splendid achievements have remained the privileges of about one-fifth of mankind and at times facilitated the process of continuing the disparities between the developed and the underdeveloped parts of the globe. Whether it is only fashionable to categorise some countries as 'developing' and some others as 'underdeveloped' or such a classification is a proof of deep research and analysis, is for the experts to ponder, the fact remains that most countries are undeveloped and should regard themselves as one lot. Collectively, they sould guard themselves against giving their hearts away and ensure that in the name of development they would not be encouraging policies and processes which, firstly, will keep them as distant from the developed world and secondly, will create new imbalances and/or strengthen traditional imbalances amongst their own people.

Deprivation and want are the basic characteristics of undeveloped societies. In specific terms, these socicties and nations are haunted by poverty, unemployment, ill-health, illiteracy (not ignorance as is generally believed) and lack of infrastructure! Destitution, disease and malnutrition are the order of the day and susceptibility to the irrational and obscurantist influences is ramarkably high. Tradition and custom are deep-rooted and, as in the case of the Indian society, can lead more to fragmentation that co-existence of a variety of ways of life. Survival is the guiding principle and there can be times when the law of the jungle is very much in evidence as social groups tend to compete with one another to hog as much share of the development as possible. There is plenty of competition but no competitiveness and competence is in short or no supply. Worse still, every developing society throws up its own articulate elite which is reluctant to part with its advantageous position and can bave stakes in maintaining the *status quo* and hence can sabotage both policy of change and its implementation. Developing societies also have an irrepressible urge to take short-cuts to development which lead to wrong policies, muddled priorites and irrelevant models being adopted. They are prone to throw up crude froms of governance, dictatorship of party or person, personality cults and military rule. Above all, suspension of fundamental rights and liberties always looms large over a developing society as we witnessed during the Internal Emergency imposed by the late Mrs. Indira Gandhi in the mid-seventies.

But it would be wrong to suppose that undeveloped and developing societies are totally devoid of positive inputs. The family — the basic and near-perfect social unit that the early man established in harmony with Nature — is still very strong and continues to thrive all over the poor parts of the world — in fact, the poor survive because they have a family to bank upon and to draw sustenance and strength from. Blatant individualism is rare and people are less self-centred. Empathy and compassion do operate up to a point, i.e., till survival or identity are not threatened, thus giving rise to neighbourhood loyalties. The milieu in general is fairly secular and, if styles or worship are not violated, tempers rarely come to the boiling point. Because people's aspirations are high they are prepared to work for a better living and motivation building is not a problem if the gains and rewards of the efforts are tangible, quick and add to the physical quality of life. Women, though not legally and socially empowered (a sad fact which should be rectified forthwith), are already skilled in various jobs and are competent to take domestic decisions and manage local affairs. The rate of saving is fairly high and does not universally go into unproductive spending on gold — this seems to be a dubious distinction of the Indian society.

Unfortunately or inadvertently as the case might have been a comprehensive amalgam was generally lost sight of in the post-Second World War models of development that were shoved down the throat of many a developing country or very cleverly marketed. The blatant emphasis on growth during the fifties and the misleading adherence to the norm of per capita growth and per capita gross domestic product created division between sections of the same society leading to internal strife and violence. The physical quality of life index which was adopted to neutralise the inequality in share of development remained ineffective because physical quality of life, for most societies had to be defined only as satisfaction of basis needs of survival; the quality of survial and the possibilities of empowerment and enrichment were given the back seat. Resource literacy as a paradigm of development won acceptance only very recently when the so-called progressive societies felt some guilt for the depletion of natural resource they had been a party to but in practice it has meant sermons to those people who have not drastically tempered with Nature and if they have done so only when there was no other way of survival. In fact, we can, in India itself, witness the confusion set in motion by the inability to weigh these models in the perspective of the more pertinent needs of the undeveloped sections society and their fulfilment as top priority.

Humanism in socio-economic milieu will have to be more of an approach and attitude than a comprehensive system of thinking or an economic and political ideology. It should be based on experience and intuition and have as its basic tenet inherent faith in the goodness of man and his desire to prosper through honest work and noble means. The secular credentials of such a humanist approach should be beyond doubt. Rather than delving deep into the abyss of known and unknown history in search of roots and justifications of the humanism we want to prevail today we must develop the confidence that the various attempts to justify the ways of God to man will offer scant justification for the ways of man to man in the millennium to come. Humanism should also have a strong element of praticality and should not fight shy of material goals and gains. Humanism and humanist in a developing society should never try to justify or rationalise, even by implication, prevailing poverty and inequality. While they should always attack everything that is irrational, obscurantist and fundamentalist and may amount to basic affront to human dignity, the humanist should display exemplary tolerance and patience in dealing with lay people in the name of case, class, religion, cult, language or geography, the humanists should imagine a broad mainstream of society and try to accommodate as many members of the society as possible into that middle layer. Gaps between rich and poor, clean and corrupt, noble and pagan, civilised and barbarian, advanced and backward, learned and illiterate, masters and servants can be effectively bridged only by broadening the centre of the chasm and not by replacing one by the other. The more recent nomenclatures of the capitalist and proletarin leaders and the led, reactionaries and revolutionaries, rural and urban, landed and landless organised and disorganised, north and south, imperial and colonised too will have to disappear gradually from the primary vocabulary of Humanists because these are in effect divisive though smart and pointed.

Numeric fractions, simple arithmetic tell us can be compatible only by having a common denominator. Humanism, to prevail and flourish, should look for the highest common multiple in a developing social scenario. Secular pluralism should not be a stance but an inbuilt trait of humanism. It goes without saying that humanism and humanists will have unshakeable faith in democracy and in matters of economics would insist of providing the basic needs of employment, shelter, protection sustenance, health, education and communication for the whole population before the other aspects of economic growth are applied and achievement on those proudly flaunted. If pluralism will guide the socio-political process in a developing society decentralisation and entrepreneurship will form the mainstay of economy. In issues rising out of creed, caste, gender, equality, mutual respect and affirmative action wherever necessary should be the obvious pointers. In environment-related matters, humanism and humanists will support neither the arrogance of conquering Nature nor the naivete of surrendering to it — but the courageous scientific way of understanding the methods and processes of Nature with a view to expediting them for better living conditions for man and more elegant conservation of Nature's richness. Should we embrace and practise the above guidelines humanism will not be reduced to the 'naked new born babe' in Macbeth striding the blasts of winter as it is forced to do at present.

This may sound simplistic and totally pragmatic, without even a pretence of philosophical discourse. True, but one look at the agenda should suffice to prove that the simplicity is only beacuse the practice of the above progamme would entail a fair measure of unlearning on the part of those who really call the shots. This lot is difficult to teach and stubborn in its resistance to change. Social scientists, champions of individual freedom and exercise of free will, protagonists of the free economy and free market, protectors of the arts and literatures and salesmen of *nirvāṇa* will attack it as one man. Questions like 'how basic are the basic needs?' and 'can equality be truly possible and/or desirable?' will be asked and the already privileged sections which have infiltrated the policy-making and implementation machinery will spare no effort in torpedoing the whole endeavour. Simple? Yes. But a demanding tall order nevertheless which will be the acid test of our conviction, dedication and perseverance to be reflected in the collective will.

My presentation could be dubbed simplistic for one more reason. I have been, not totally inadvertently, overemphasising the materialistic side of progress and have avoided the finer deeper side of man. Would the satisfaction of needs and freedom from want necessarily lead to a more refined human being or would it not vent the base in man as delinquents and dropouts in the most developed societies testify with the violent inhuman treatment they meet out fellow human beings? Wouldn't the privileged members of a materially fulfilled society lose the basic desire for work and forget the honest sweet of one's brow? Such questions however should not deter one from the materialistic approach because, as statistics have shown time and again, the proportion of errands and delinquents is generally constant, like the gender ratio under all conditions. That man is, by the virtue of being human, basically good, positive, benevolent and turns to grab and rob only when he sees no decent ways of attaining freedom from want, should be the first commandment of humanism. We have to go back to the pre-fall-from-the-Garden of Eden preception of ourselves to be vibrant humanists, leaving behind all the fearsome visions of ourselves as displayed in the debate over cloning when even the most learned asked questions like wouldn't cloning open up the possibilities of creating innumerable villains like Hitler, to be rejoindered by the possibility of creating innumerable Gandhis or Christs. Humanism is not about the war between Hitlers and Gandhis but about the eradication of the need to have either of them.

Be that as it may, I have hesitation in pleading guilty of a simplistic approach to a complex issue I owe this modesty to two great minds hailing from nearby. Rabīndranāth Tagore, when he wrote his prayer "Into that heaven of Freedom my Father let my Country awake" was even more simplistic. He asked for a world "where the mind is without fear and the head is held high. Where knowledge is free" and there are no narrow domestic walls. As simple as you will have it. But the second great mind I am proudly indebted to is the late Shankar Guha Niyogi whom I call the Christ of Chattisgarh. When he wrote his manifesto *Hamare Sapanonka Chattisgarh* he supplemented the abstractions of Tagore with some simple this-worldly goals. He wanted a heaven with drinking water, irrigation, jobs, fair agricultural prices, a hospital for every village, schools (with the school master present), land and home for all families. This Chattisgarh would have no capitalism and no exploitation, where the small peasants and workers would be their own masters. Most simple once again.

I submit, in all humility, that, put together, the prayer and the manifesto would amount to a comprehensive agenda for Humanism in a Developing Social Scenario.

Humanism in a Developing Society
With Special Reference to Scientific Humanism

Tandra Patnaik

INDIAN society is passing through the most critical phase of its history. For centuries it has upheld its own identity despite the onslaughts of alien cultures and values. But during the last decade the rapid progress of information technology has reduced the world into a global village. The process of globalisation and liberalisation has almost caught us unawares. We are forced to think along the line of what is globally acceptable. The concept of a global village is no doubt a noble concept — while in practice it is nothing but permeation of a culture which focuses man as a consumer, as a product and as an object, to say the least. It is a progressive culture of dehumanisation. There is a large section of Indian elites, who remains totally complacent laying the blame on science and scientific progress. We have reached a stage where setting the clock back is an impossibility. Nor lamenting about the erosion of the great Indian culture of spirituality is of any help. My task in this paper is to examine the concept of man *vis-a-vis* the ideas fostered by modern science and to seek a viable alternative model for the future society.

Before I proceed with my task I would like to pay some attention to the two key words used in the title of my paper — 'developing society' and 'humanism'. A society and civilisation as a whole are believed to be always in the process of development. So what is so new about the word 'developing society'? It is a word coined by the rich and powerful nations with economic and technological progress to distinguish themselves from those nations which are not so privileged. It is rather a soft and decent synonym of the term 'underdeveloped'. India is one of such countries which fits into the category of 'developing' nation, — a nation which depends on developed nations for technical know-how and financial help. But along with economic and technological dependence our society is showing certain amount of eagerness to absorb the culture of the developed nations. In this sense, India of the 1990s truly is a developing society. But what is the need for humanism in such a society? To answer this question we have to understand what humanism means.

Humanism is a much used term; every theory, every ideology seems to lay claim on this word without always clearly demarcating its boundary. This makes the task of elucidating the implications of the term 'humanism' mandatory. It should be admitted at the outset that the term does not stand for a single theory or hypothesis. Broadly speaking, it symbolises a shifting of the centre of gravity from supernaturalism to naturalism, from transcendental to the existing, from abstrations, to a living reality. In brief, it indicates the place of man at the centre of everything. Its roots can be traced to the philosophical traditions of India, China, Greece and Rome. The faith of some ancient systems in the potentialities of man was somehow submerged by the overwhelming sway of religion in the medieval period, but it resurfaced during renaissance. Renaissance humanism aimed at rekindling faith in man and his power. Two distinctive feature of this phase of humanism were self-confidence and anti-authoritarianism. The scope of such self-confidence was enhanced by a series of scientific discoveries. The power of science gadually transformed man into a conqueror who hoped to keep the universe under his control. But the self-confidence infused by science itself proved to be self-defeating. It glorifed value-neutrality, a-morality, mechanism and materialism. The method of formal reasoning replaced value-based reasoning. The word, the 'society', the 'environment' which are key terms in sociological analysis of man were treated as *sui-generis* and self-regulating systems and ultimately it was claimed that the project of human sciences is not to constitute man but to dissolve him. So what stemmed from humanism ultimately led to the dehumanisation and de-centering of 'man'. In recent times, humanism, therefore is anchored in a new connotation. It now refers to a 'self-confidence' which arises from achieving a balance between the 'inner' and 'outer' needs of life. Winning over nature is no more the goal, but winning over savage and pathetic tendencies of man assumes more importance. The new humanism is based on understanding of man as a being in relation to the rest of the environment. The implications of the term humanism can be best summed up in the words of Julian Huxley:

> Such humanism is necessarily unitary instead of dualistic, affirming the unity of mind and body, universal instead of particularist, affirming the continuity of man with the rest of life, and life with the rest of the universe; naturalistic instead of supernaturalist, affirming the unity of the spiritual and the material.... Humanism thinks in terms of directional process instead of in those static mechanism, in terms of quality and diversity as well as quantity and unity. It will have nothing to do with absolutes, including absolute morality, absolute perfection, absolute authority, but insists that we can find standards to which actions and aims can be properly related.[1]

So we have noted that is the term humanism has a history of its own. Its form has changed in different stages of human development. Besides, humanisms has been judged from varied angles. So we have multiple forms of humanism — Existentialistic humanism, Marxist humanism, spiritual humanism radical humanism — some of these are still significant. Some have lost their glamour. But all of them offer priority to the concept of man and his autonomy. I have chosen Huxley's definition, for in the present context we are more worried about the dehumanisation stemming from scientific view of the universe. And Huxley is a pioneer scientist anf confirmed humanist.

Science and Man

We have noted that science and the world-view projected by it, has been held responsible for the dominance of a culture which decentres

---

1. J. Huxley, *The Humanist Frame*, George Allen and Unwin, London, 1961, p. 4.

man. Many people call it the tyranny of science. But before we pass the entire buck on science for all the woes of the present state of affairs, we should stop and probe a bit on what the twentieth-century scientists have to say about scientific view of the universe. The tyrannical picture of science which decentres human person, objectifies him and his universe is the story of nineteenth-century attitude of science. The cocksureness and the feeling of triumph which was the characteristic feature of the previous century is already replaced by a sense of humility and reconciliation by the modern scientist. Especially in the field of physics and biology, the scientists have felt the limitations of relying on the 'external' aspect of life. They have become acutely aware of the urgency to understand man and his 'inner' being.

In this context it is necessary to examine of the recent views of scientists regarding the inadequacy and limitations of their world-view. This will give us some idea about finding out the solution to the malady of the present generation. Pere Teilhard de Chardin's remarks about physics is worth noting. He says:

> The time has come to realise that an interpretation of the universe — even a positivist one — remains unsatisfying unless it convers the interior as well as the exterior of things, mind as well as matter. The true physics is that which will, one day, achieve the inclusion of man in his wholeness in a coherent picture of the world.[2]

Julian Huxley in the similar vein, explains the new attitude of biological sciences,

> In the light of our present knowledge, man's most comprehensive aim is seen not as survival, not as numerical increase, not as increased complexity of organisation, or increased control over his environment, but as greater fulfilment — the fuller realisation of more possibilities by

2. Pere Teithard de Chardin, *The Phenomenon of Man* , Collins, London, 1989, pp. 35-6.

> human species collectively and more of its component members individually.[3]

The new awareness expressed by the modern scientists help us to realise that the present human predicament is not caused by the culture of science. Rather it gives us the hope that we can be in a position to have a society based on humanistic principle without throwing our hands in despair. Such a model was offered to us by Nehru in his book, *The Discovery of India*. He prefers to call it Scientific Humanism.

Scientific Humanism

Nehru pinpoints that the problem of any society, at any stage of its growth is the balancing between the 'inner' an 'outer' aspects of individual life and adjustment of relation betwen the individuals and the society.

> The real problems for me remain the problems of individual and social life, of harmonious living, of a proper balancing of an individual's inner and outer life, of an adjustment of relations between the individuals and the groups, of continuous becoming, something better and higher of social development, of the ceaseless adventure of man.[4]

Nehru's formulation of the basic social problem admits of a perennial scope for conflict at two levels of a person's social existence. In the individual plane, the conflict is between the 'inner' and 'outer' dimensions; in the social plane it is between a man's individual and group interest. The resolution of the first problem holds the key to the resolution of the second. And for this, we have to accept the importance of both — science and philosophy/religion. In spite of Nehru's immense faith in science and technology as the catalyst for the development of a nation state like India, he did not overlook the

---

3. J. Huxley, "The Evolution of Life", in *Evolution after Darwin*, Chicago University Centennial, Vol. I, 1959, p.17.
4. J. Nehru, *The Discovery of India*, Oxford University Press, New Delhi, 1983, p. 31.

importance of spiritual quest. He admits

> . . . some faith is necessary in the things of spirit which are beyond the scope of our physical world, some reliance on moral, spiritual and idealistic conceptions. Or else we have no anchorage, no objectives and purposes in life.[5]

This emphasis on a harmony between the body and mind, 'inner' and 'outer' urges of man, leads him to formulate the conception of scientific humanism. He says,

> we have to therefore function in the line with the highest ideals of the age we live in. . . . These ideals may be classed under two heads: humanism and scientific spirit . . . there is a growing synthesis between humanism and scientific spirit resulting in a kind of scientific humanism.[6]

It is worth noting here that Nehru tries to incorporate the value of science in a society in terms of the spirit and temperament that a scientific analysis fosters. He sees this as a "way of life, a process of thinking, a method of acting and associating with our own fellowmen".[7] This is best reflected in man's indomitable spirit of adventure, the yearning for the truth, anti-dogmatism and openness of attitude towards life and environment. It is the spirit of objectivity, dynamism and flexibility. This temperament is not opposed to man's yearning for the inner truth — hence it leads to a form of humanism. For him humanism implies the conception of 'man' in its totality along with the multiple dimensions of his personality. Man is neither a pure body nor a pure mind, neither an isolated individual nor a cog in the wheel of social organism. It is an ideal which aims at finding a balance. Nehru says, "we have to discover a balance between the body and the spirit and between man as a part of nature and man as a part of society".[8] He must not lose his

---

5. J. Nehru, *The Discovery of India*, p. 513.
6. *Ibid.*, p. 558.
7. *Ibid.*, p. 512.
8. *Ibid.*, p. 561.

dignity and the essence of his being, for he in neither a puppet in the hands of nature nor a slave of the transcendental Being. Therefore, Nehru reaches a very significant conclusion which summarises his position on humanism. "...one may not lose faith in man. God we may deny but what hope is left for us if deny man and thus reduce everything to futility".[9]

Humanism Beyond Twentieth Century

Nehru's brand of scientific humanism, in no sense, is a utopia or romance. It is an ideal which can be transformed into practice. The hard-core scientists have already realised that science in its true spirit cannot be pursued if they neglect the dignity and potentialities of man. Yet the recent malady of Indian society does not emanate from the tyranny of science. It is rather the tyranny of the culture of technology. Science, as is well-known, has two dimensions — science has **lucifera** (light) and science as **fructifera** (fruit). Both of them are intimately related. Every scientific discovery when transformed in technology endows man with power and power leads to control of nature enabling man to condition his life and enviornment. So man is naturally attracted to science as a fruit, i.e., scientific knowledge transformed into technology. There is nothing wrong with technology — but there is surely something wrong with the philosophy that technology fosters. It is the philosophy of power that crushes under its feet anything that stands for human dignity. It preaches to close the 'inner window' and divide the world into 'developed' and 'developing' societies in terms of technological advancement. Its ugly bi-product is the culture of consumerism, which reduces man into a capital, resource or else as object. So Nehru's scientific humanism needs certain modifications, if it has to serve as a model of the developing society of India. Nehru perhaps had some idea about the nature of things come. In a note of warning he says,

> ... the progress of science unconnected with and isolated

---

9. J. Nehru, *The Discovery of India*, p. 479

> from moral discipline and ethical considerations, will lead to the concentration of power and terrible instruments of destruction which it has made, in the hands of evil and selfish men, seeking domination of others — and thus destruction of its own achievements.[10]

This to a large extent is the predicament world at large and Indian society in particular is facing. Not only we live in constant fear of destruction, we are feeling inwardly impoverished and empty in an environment of wealth, pleasure and power. The inner emptiness has made most our people smitten with ennui and boredom arising out a materialistic *weltanschauung*. The predicament of modern age was foreseen by our sages of yore. *Śvetāśvatara Upaniṣad* describes it in following words:

> Even though men may (through their technical skill) roll up the space like a piece of leather, still there will be no end of sorrow for them without the realisation of the luminous one within.[11]

Fortunately for us, this is the clue to the solution of the maladies of the present society, within our own tradition. Indian culture has always tried to keep a balance between the 'external' and 'internal', applied science and spiritualism with more emphasis on the realisation of the inner spirit of the man. But average modern Indian has some sort of aversion towards our cultural heritage. Thanks to the consistent efforts of our philosophical and religious *puṇḍits*. They have projected successfully Indian culture as primarily and essentially spiritual. Besides, for long Indians have indoctrinated to think in their line and to believe that technological progress is a bad word. The eagerness of the present generation to turn to the culture of consumerism seems to be a reaction against such indoctrination. It is high time, we look at our culture without a bias. We must realise that our ancient tradition believed in balancing between the external and internal needs. If India has *ādhyātmya*

---

10. J. Nehru, *The Discovery of India*, p. 479.
11. *Śvetāśvatara Upaniṣad*, VI.20.

śāstra to boast of, we should no less be proud of our treatises on *artha-śāstra* (politics/economics), *Vāstu-śāstra* (architecture), *āyurveda* (medicine) and *rasāyana-śāstra*. All these disciplines deal with applied science. Our ancient sages realised as we do realise to day that

> a man who is victim of economic circumstances, and who is hedged and restricted by struggle to live can very rarely achieve inner consciousness of a higher degree.[12]

So let us learn from our tradition and apply rational genius in combining the spirit of progress and human dignity.

---

12. J. Nehru, *An Autobiography*, Oxford University Press, New Delhi, 1981, p. 379.

Humanism and Phenomenology of Crisis

Sharad Deshpande

WHAT humanism is and what it is not, and who is or who is not a humanist are difficult questions to answer. This is because a peculiar sentiment, which may be termed as a humanist sentiment, is often confused with an alleged philosophical or quasi-philosophical doctrine which is titled as humanism. So the first point I wish to make is: that having of a peculiar sentiment — the humanist sentiment — either in terms of equality of all men or universal brotherhood, or for man's uniqueness, or his privileged position in the overall scheme of nature, is one thing; but to have a fully articulate philosophical doctrine which would go under the name of humanism, is quite another. I am inclined to think that all the popular versions of humanism (or whatever view or views which go under this title) are quasi-philosophical doctrines based on this peculiar humanist sentiment. Protagoras, in the Western tradition, may be seen as the first to express this humanist sentiment when he proclaimed that man is a measure of all things. There are countless many including saints, mystics, and poets, who have similarly expressed this sentiment in various ways. But if we wish to treat humanism as a full-blown philosophical doctrine then a mere sentimental basis may not be enough. With this caution, I believe, we will be able to take care of all such attempts to read humanism (as a full-blown philosophical theory) in various texts — philosophical or literary — which express the humanist sentiment rather than humanism as a philosophical doctrine.

The second point I wish to make concerns the humanist discourse with which we claim familiarity. No doubt our claim is justified in terms of our information about the humanist literature, humanist writers and the like. But the fact to be recognised is that the humanist discourse is essentially European and that it operates within the broad framework of modernity. It is, in other words, a Modernist Discourse. The recognition of this historical fact would be the second step towards averting at least some confusions relating humanism and civilisation or cultural diversities. As it is well-known, the modernist discourse of humanism presents a world-view, in which man is placed at the centre by virtue of his, and only his, having a capacity for emancipation. This world-view is presented in the cluster of different theses which have formed a great deal of history of ideas concerning various dimensions of man's existence such as religion, morality, language, art, science and culture. Whatever the dimension, the humanist thesis resists any temptation to reduce 'being human' to 'being an object in nature' on the ground that human existence is unique in nature. This thesis, in its various presentations, has always been deeply anchored in the history of European civilisation and it represents the tensions which the European civilisation felt and various crisis it underwent during different phases of its history.

Recognition of this fact, i.e., the humanist discourse represents the tensions which the European civilisation felt during various phases of its history, would enable one to seriously question one of widespread assumptions about humanism that it offers a universal doctrine which cuts across all cultural diversities. At the outset, this assumption seems uncontrovertible, because of its simplicity. Who would deny the uniqueness or the privileged position of man in the overall scheme of nature? Who would ordinarily deny that all men are equal in some sense or the other? But on a closer examination one finds this assumption, i.e., humanism as a universal doctrine or philosophy highly problematic. This is because the very concepts of man, and nature, and their interrelationship is conceived differently in various cultures and civilisations. This historical fact makes it clear that there is no such or there cannot be any such single or universal doctrine of humanism which is or can be valid for all civilisations and cultures comprising them. Had there been such a universal doctrine of humanism, it would obliterate the culture specificity of man-nature relationship. As a matter of fact, diversities among different cultures, at a deeper level are due to, among other things, the different ways in which this relationship is conceived. The differences in the conception of man-nature relationship and the corresponding conceptual spaces they create are due to complex interaction between different elements which constitue any given culture. The contemporary humanist discourse in which we wish to participate has a long history which dates back to the long drawn Renaissance movement of the thirteenth to the seventeenth-century Europe. Artistically, Renaissance was an assertion of the power of an individual genius and philosophically, it was a celebration of the rediscovery of the classical humanism, of belief in the power of man as man rather than in his dependence on God and his impotence before Nature. The humanist thesis in this period of its history, is largely an outcome of the emergence of New Science. It sought to provide hegemony to modern or the new science as one of the legitimate elements of society. The emergence of the modern, i.e., Galilean Science required, for its own possibility and also validity, a certain theoretical position or a world-view about man and nature. The new science with its distinctive methodology required an autonomous human being who would be critical of everything and especially of the authority of the church as far as the explanation of nature is concerned. Descartes' *cogito* which is vested with the power of doubting everything until it reaches certainty may be seen as epitomising this autonomous individual as self-sufficient in knowledge and action, which makes modern science possible. But paradoxically as it were, the concept of autonomous (or self-sufficient) individual and the conception of nature as mechanistic did not prove to be compatible since the concept of an autonomous individual also implied that such an autonomous individual has a free will. Thus the humanist discourse with which we claim familiarity represents inner tensions between the Renaissance conception of an autonomous individual in such domains as Religion and Morality on the one hand and the understanding of nature as mechanistic system on the other. These kinds of theoretical tensions which the Renaissance and the post-Renaissance European civilisation felt can be illustrated by giving various examples from different domains such as politics and philosophy. The point which I wish to make is that once we recognise that the modern humanist discourse is basically European, the other non-European cultures are under no obligation to take the European version of humanism as universally valid. I wish to argue that each culture has its own humanist outlook and humanism as world-view. This point can be discussed in further details as to how each culture views man in relation to nature and *vice-versa* and how cultures differ on the issue of the centrality of man. Understanding such differences is not an easy task. What one would need to know would be the specific categories in terms of which each culture articulates its own humanist discourse. But many times the categories in terms of which the European humanism finds its articulation are straight away borrowed to 'read' humanism in non-European cultures. In the Indian context, if one wishes to evolve a humanist discourse a considerable amount of anthropological and sociological studies would be a prerequisite rather than taking a recourse to the metaphysical systems such as Adviata Vedānta. I have great doubts about the noe-Vedāntin's efforts to fashion humanist discourse on the metaphysical doctrines of classical Advaita Vedānta. This point can also be discussed in further details such as whether the metaphysical monism of Advaita Vedānta can justify social inequalities. My contention is that the humanist discourse of Indian origin will have to be evolved around the socio-political and religious ethos of the people of India rather than the underlying metaphysics of a particular orientation. The socio-political and also the religious ethos which was evolved, say, out of the Brāhmaṇical and the Buddhist encounters, or out of various *smṛti* traditions would provide the space in which the Humanist discourse of Indian origin would operate. In other words, one will have to locate various crisis the Indian society (if there is any such unitary entity) has undergone during various phases of its history. In fact, understanding and assessment of crisis would be the first step towards formulating the Humanist thesis. Although in this paper I have not been able to specify fully or even in outline, the foundations of humanism as a philosophical theory, I feel that the concept of crisis will be a foundational notion for any philosophical account of humanism. The term-crisis in its Greek etymology, means choice or selection, judgement or trial, crisis or critical moment. Husserl, as we know, is perhaps the first philosopher who has fully exploited the notion of crisis as constitutive idea in Human

Sciences. He uses the term crisis in both the later sense. He uses it to refer to a problem constitutive of one or more areas of human concerns such as reason or rationality, science and method, philosophy and psychology, the relation between objective knowledge and subjectivity. Taking a clue from Husserlian employment of the notion of crisis as explanatory category to characterise Human Sciences, I suggest that the humanist discourse which seek to transcend the humanist sentiment into a full-fledged philosophical world-view called humanism, does presuppose the notion of crisis in a very significant way.

One crucial theme in the phenomenology of crisis or of critical moment would be that man is a self-interpreting animal. The Heideggerian notion of interpretation would be a key term for the humanist thesis because it seeks to bridge up the gap between man's experience of reality on the hand and reality *qua* reality on the other. The hermeneutical philosophers talk about the interpretative function of human mind in the sense that to interpret is to invest phenomena with meaning. In fact, the concept of a fully developed human agency demands that such an agency is capable of interpretative function or having interpretation as a mode of knowing. To interpret is to be engaged in creative appropriation of the phenomena presented to, or brought before the human mind in its capacity as conscious agent and contemplative observer. Those of us who wish to develop the humanist thesis in Indian context may find these two notions, i.e., crisis and interpretation useful.

Spiritual Humanism in the Bhagavad Gītā

Narayana Chandra Padhi

'HUMANISM' has acquired enormous significance in the present developing social scenario. Considered in a wider perspective, it involves many crucial issues like human person, human situation, human aspirations, etc. As such, different forms of humanism have come to the focus. In what follows, I shall restrict myself to a form of humanism within the purview of the *Bhagavad Gītā*. The bone of my contention in this paper will be that the purpose of the *Gītā* is the divinisation of man only, though 'divinisation' need not necessarily have a transcendental import. The point I want to drive at here is that the humanism of the *Gītā*, viewed by some as spiritual humanism, gives a proper account of the term 'humanism' itself.

I

At the outset, it is necessary to take a bird's eye-view on the different forms of humanism with a view to distinguish the humanism of *Gītā*. The naturalistic and scientific humanism have restricted the term to the realm of nature only. The scientific humanist studies man from biological standpoint only. For a scientific humanist like Pt. Jawaharlal Nehru man, as the result of natural forces, is to be judged scientifically and not metaphysically. Empirical, not transcendental considerations constitutes the only criterion of humanism. More or less, radical humanism goes to the extent of defining man in terms of certain biological elements and physical laws.

As against this, the existentialist, emphasising upon human predicament gives a dogmatic view. Olson states the existentialism position as follows:

> Frustration, insecurity and painful striving are the inescapable lot of human mind, and the only life worth living is one in which this fact is squarely faced; for, if the existentialists are right, a life of frustration, insecurity, and painful striving itself generates values, and the values so generated are the only ones actually realisable and genuinely worthy of human pursuit.[1]

The centre of the existential situation is man itself. Jean Paul Sartre stretches it to the extreme view that human body is a concrete centre of reference. The things in the world are oriented towards the body and reveal it. Placing the existentialist position of Sartre, Blackham writes:

> All the things which I habitually use are organised in my world and indicate my bodily presence which gives them their place and meaning. Similarly, the great public places and services presuppose and refer to the bodies that frequent and use them.[2]

The purpose of giving a reference to the above-mentioned forms of humanism is not to state its historical development. The only purpose is to show that a proper assessment of the term cannot be made with reference to human body or the human predicament only. Rather, this can be expected of in the line of thinking reflected in the *Gītā*. While the humanistic trends are one-sided and dogmatic, the *Gītā* proposes a comprehensive picture of humanism.

II

The *Bhagavad Gītā* essentially incorporates the ethical teaching

---

1. G. Olson Robert, *An Introduction to Existentialism*, Dover Publications, Inc. New York, 1962, p.14.
2. H.J. Blackham, — *Six Existentialist Thinkers*, Routledge & Kegan Paul, London, 1961, p. 119.

meant for giving a rational foundation for a perfect human living. It places a model of humanity also with a view to instill this ideal for a spiritual life, which is far removed from the nasty selfish existence. At the outset, a reference may be made to the categorisation of existing beings to *deva*, *dānava* and *mānava*.[3] This categorisation aims at showing that the human beings alone can be termed in any of the three ways depending upon their actions. Through irrational unrighteous actions man degrades himself to the level of devils and elevate his attitudes through just actions and righteous living. Thus, *Gītā* emphasises upon the rational foundation of human living and issues a note of warning in the event of the degradation and decay of this foundation. It says that whenever righteousness is in jeopardy, the exploitation of the nobles goes to the extreme and the forces of evil have their sway.[4]

The concern of the *Bhagavad Gītā* is clearly indicated in its treatment of the most compelling problem, i.e., the problem of human suffering, which also constitutes the major issue for the Indian philosophical thinking. The problem of evil, which is one of the arresting issues both in the Indian and Western philosophies of religion figures prominently in the *Gītā*. To the star question of Arjuna regarding the genesis of evil, Lord Kṛṣṇa points his finger at the bad elements in the human beings.[5] The problem of theodicy is dealt with in a simpler way. The so-called notions like heaven and hell do not refer to any supramundane or supernatural existence. They are the normal human experiences. Evil is nothing but the resulting conceptions of human anger, infatuation, etc. Thus evil is not due to the fall from the Divine grace, nor is it due to the violation of the design preordained by God. In the words of St. Augustine "All evil is either sin or the punishment of sin." The *Gītā*, which notably subscribes to the *karma* doctrine returns reward and punishment to human action only. Leaving aside the consideration of moral evil, natural evil or physical human suffering is not due to any extrasensory element. This is purely a human affair within the

---

3. *The Bhagavad Gītā* (*BG*), XVI.
4. *Ibid.*, IV.7.
5. *Ibid.*, III.39.

human situation. According to the *Gītā*, experiences like pleasure and pain are due to te contact of sense-organs with the objects. This point has been more elaborately discussed in the thirteenth chapter of the *Gītā* where human body has been considered as a field of experience (*kṣetra*). Commenting upon this *śloka* Śaṅkara says that human body, known as a field of experience, is subject to changes from time to time. The possible reason is that the human body enjoys or suffers due to its past activities

> *kṣatra tranat kṣaranat kṣetravad va asmin karmaphala nirvṛtteh kṣetram iti evaṁ abhidhīyate kathyate* [6]

Here, of course, the difficulty is to accommodate the transcendental element like the ultimate experiencer (Puruṣottama) within the conceptual framework of humanism.

Another point that strikes us most is the possibility of freedom from suffering. This is the issue which is concerned with the religious way of life. In the ultimate sense it means liberation. The most pertinent issue here is, what is the way out of the human suffering? It is the belief that man has to suffer as long as there is the feeling of pleasure and pain (*saṁsāra*) or as long as man goes on moving in the cycle of birth and rebirth. What, then is the way out of this impasse? It is worthwhile to note that here too the *Gītā* falls back upon the human endeavour. This is known as the path of action (*karma-yoga*) which is manifested in three forms: *karma, jñāna* and *bhakti*. All these are included within the scope of human effort. Of course, total surrender at the feet of the Lord has been highlighted as the last resort. That, however, does not contradict the humanistic outlook of the *Gītā*. Rather, it can be argued that such a recommendation is there to instil a sense of hope at the time of despair. But, what is more important to observe here is the emphasis given on *Buddhiyoga*.[7] This has been dignified in the *Gītā* as the controller of all the *yogas*. Though *Buddhiyoga* may not be considered at par with *karma*, *jñāna* and *bhakti*, yet it plays a distinct role so far as the teachings of the *Gītā* is concerned. It is, so

---

6. *BG*, *Śāṅkara Bhāṣya*, XIII.1. Gita Press, Gorakhpur.
7. *BG,* X.10, further see II.49.

to say, the controller of all the *yogas*. *Buddhiyoga* works like a regulative principle controlling and gearing human action in its proper way. Particular reference may be made here to a noted commentator, Bairagi Mishra.[8] Bairagi Mishra offers justificatory notes in favour of the thesis that so far as the *Gītā* is concerned, *Buddiyoga* is treated as the Lord himself, Reference to *Buddhiyoga* has been made here to vindicate the role of *buddhi* (human intellect) in the course of human action.

So far so good. But, what about *niṣkāma-karma* or the *anāsakti-yoga* itself? It might appear difficult to accommodate this *yoga* in the scheme of the humanism. The problem is, if the *Bhagavad Gītā* asks us to renounce the fruits of action and to lead a detached life withdrawing ourselves from the experiences of pleasure and pain, how can *anāsakti-yoga* be called as the life-affirming? Does it not run counter to the philosophy of humanism itself? This is an important issue no doubt. In fact, this is the common place objection against *niṣkāma-karmayoga*. To my mind, this does not pose a serious threat to the humanism of the *Gītā*.

In order to understand the rational foundation of the *anāsakti-yoga* one has to consider the central point of the *Gītā* itself. The central point of the *Gītā*, as it appears, is the purposive human individual who wills to act in every situation. The individual encounters a moral crisis at a particular juncture of life. He has to interact with the world to seek a solution and yet has to carve out his own destiny by the creative power of his will. The gamut of discussion then turns down to the human situation . However, the *Gītā* cautions against egoism or pettishness of outlook which is, the resultant conception of too much of emphasis laid on human body. Human life is neither to be viewed within the narrow sphere of Jung's animus or anima aspect, nor is it to be viewed as a selfish nasty existence. Human life is to be judged in a broader perspective of social existence. Highest social order is nothing but spiritual order. Reference may be made her to the *Īśa Upaniṣad* which speaks of realisation of one's own self in others and *vice-versa*. In the

---

8. Bairagi Mishra's commentary (Oriyā) — *Bairagi Mishra Granthavali.*

similar vein the *Gītā* says that the aim of all the *yoga* is *lokasaṁgraha* or *sarvabhūta hite rataḥ*. For the realisation of this end what is required is self-sacrifice. In this sense *anāsakti-yoga* constitutes rational foundation of the type of humanism stipulated in the *Gītā*.

III

The problem now confronts us here is to give a justification to the spiritualistic or holistic element which figures so prominently in the *Bhagavad Gītā*. It is well-known that the *Gītā* drives at the point of divinisation of the entire human existence. That the spiritual *weltanschauung* of the *Gītā* is at the root of this holism is well-known. The difficulty is, to accommodate humanism within the conceptual framework of spiritualism.

One of the programmes of spiritualism as Professor Mishra[9] views it, is emphasis on asceticism which is the resulting conception of "the idea of a self-conscious, self-identical, immaterial soul, the idea of a pure subject and mere spirit". According to him again, "the picture to which ascetic holds fast is an unintelligible picture. His attitude of indifference towards worldly affairs is a result of bad logic and wrong metaphysics." That the *Gītā* subscribes to this view is quite evident from the statement, "Just as a man puts-off the old worn-out garment and takes up a new one, so also the human person casts off the old body"[10] at the time of death and assumes a new body". Another significant metaphysical view is the acceptance of the omnipresence and omniscience of God. In the words of the *Bhagavad Gītā*, "I am the beginning, the continuing and the end of entire existence." And at the end of the entire discourse, the Lord say, "surrender everything to me leaving aside all your paths and I shall grant you freedom from the whirlpool of suffering".[11] What are we to do here so far as humanism is concerned? Can the humanism of the *Gītā* stand with equal vigour against the strong anti-current of spiritualism? If a human being is reduced to pure

9. G. Mishra, "Spirit, Machine and Man", *The Humanist Vision*, ed. by B. Kar, p. 45.
10. *BG*, II.22.
11. *Ibid.*, XVIII.66.

subjectivity or a mere convenient tool in the hands of the divine, then the humanism in the *Gītā* will boil down to a mere slogan only. What are we to do with it?

As it appears, the *Gītā* has been often misconstrued as the preacher of asceticism and world-denying. To my mind neither the *Gītā* advocates world-denial nor the metaphysical views affect the core concept of humanism. It is absolutely unjustified to maintain that the *Gītā* subscribes to the view of sure subjectivity. It has been discussed earlier that the significant issue is the human being, and its problems. The affirmation of the embodied individual (*dehī*) as the point of reference of all activities constitutes the core concept. One might argue here that the introduction of the concepts like *kṣetrajña*, 'the immanent controller', etc., discards the agential freedom of the individual which is the striking feature of humanism. This argument along with the 'ghost in the machine'[12] hypothesis does not seriously affect the humanism of *Gītā*. Such spiritual elements are admitted in the secondary sense only. Without contradicting the humanistic element, the *Gītā* carves out its own model with the help of the spiritual ideas. Such ideas ennoble the human individual and open up wider dimensions. Moreover, it is significant to note that the model of humanism, which reflects the human situation in a proper way may not be a pure metaphysical model nor a scientific or naturalistic model which confines human beings within the framework of natural propensities only. The model of a value-oriented life cannot be lost sight of in order to give a rational justification of human situation. Dr. Mishra, has not discarded this element from his conceptual scheme. Rather, he says:

> worldly prosperity in a social world of obligations and duties, rewards and punishments, cooperation and conformity is all that he can possibly think of attaining. In guaranteeing the continuity of social order the guarantees his own continuity; in guaranteeing the social well-being, he can ensure his own well-being. . . . A philosophy which can open up this insight is humanistic in outlook[13] viewed

12. G. Ryle, *The Concept of Mind*, chapter I.
13. G. Mishra, *op. cit.*, p. 46.

> in this way the humanism in the *Gītā* is quite humanistic as the motto of the *Gītā* is the maintenance of the social order, of course not with the explicit purpose to ensure the well-being of the individual only. To foster social well-being with a view to ensure one's own well-being is a utilitarian outlook to which the *Gītā* does not subscribe. The humanism of the *Gītā* is to be viewed in a still broader prospective. The *sumum bonum* of human life is to see everybody as one's own self.[14]

That is the *yoga*, which is otherwise known as practising mental equanimity at the individual level and realising equality in the social level—*samatvaṁ yogamuchyate*. This can be treated as God-realisation in the language of *Gītā*.

The concept of *dharma*, particularly *svadharma* needs a special mention in this context. In the spiritualistic model of humanism stipulated in the *Gītā*, *dharma* aims at the *abhyudaya* (moral upliftment) as well as *niḥeśrayasa* or the realisation of the highest ideal or God-realisation. The *Gītā* takes this concept of *dharma* as a mundane affair and points out that one who performs *dharma* regarding it as regulative principle of human existence, reaps the consequences in this life and in this body.[15] This is how *dharma* works at the level of theoretical reason.

In conclusion, it can be said that the spiritualistic *weltanschauung* of the *Gītā* refers to man in his total relationship with the reality as a single and singular whole. The holistic assertion is the assertion of an omnipresent, omniscient, omnipotent spiritual principle which manifests itself in every form: vegetative, animal and human.[16] The theoretical reason, which is the rational foundation of human existence is rather controlled by the postulates of practical reason in Kantian sense.

---

14. *BG*, XIII.27-8.
15. *Ibid.*
16. See Javdekar, *Indian Philosophical Quarterly*, 1988, Vol. X, No.4, p. 462.

Can Modern Society be Humanistic?

P.R. Bhat

Two arguments are advanced to show that certain forms of humanism is not philosophically defendable. Humanism based on the notion self which is metaphysical in nature is not possible for two reasons: The modern industrialised society forces us to have professional ethics which undermine the dignity of man. Second, the autonomy of the moral agent itself calls in question given the advancement in the sphere of biotechnology. This paper, therefore, makes a plea for respect for all forms of life. Thus, the notion of humanism has to be extended to include animals and plants.

I

Kant had made the suggestion that we should not use other individuals merely as means. That is to say, he believed that individuals have their dignity and that should not be overlooked. The autonomy of an individual along with his moral rights has to be granted by every individual. However, the modern industrialised society is quite complex. Inter-dependency is increasingly becoming the order of the day. For instance, if one segment of the society, say the workers of railways go on strike, it would take the shape of a national crisis. The same is more or less true of other sectors like, electricity supply, water supply, banking and so on. As the society advances, interdependency increases; at the industrial and social level; but anonymity and independence may increase at the individual level. To meet the challenges of man including the basic needs, we depend more and more on science and technology. Because of the mechanisation and sophistication involved in managing the public service systems and other essential services, the speicialisations have become necessary. The same is true of every sector of an industrialised society.

Putnam has spoken about the division of labour; we need to identify experts and make use of expert knowledge. No one person would be in a position to use the language of all specialised branches. This is because, the science, technology and the complex modern society force us to specialise and extend expert help to the individuals. In the villages, we no more depend on cattle for agriculture and transport. Animals are replaced by machines in the villages; and men are replaced by computers wherever in the cities. The days are of 'experts' and knowledge has become the source of money and power. As a consequence, specialisation and professionalisation has become inevitable.

Different professionals mushroom since their service is needed to the society at large. The aim of the profession is to provide efficient service: medicine, the health; education, the knowledge, legal, providing justice and so on.[1] Professionalisation is a process of demarcating the field of operation by experts and method of efficiently delivering services and goods. Professionals may be hired by the government to serve the basic needs of its citizens such as doctors, teachers and so on under the umbrella of welfare programmes. It is also possible that the government cannot meet the general requirement of the citizens and permits certain private organisations to supply the additional services and goods against a nominal charge or fee. Education itself may be professionalised and we may introduce the competitive spirit right at the start by commercialisation of edcation. It is quite natural to believe that commercialisation of education itself would make the our would be professionals to align themselves with the business propositions. An efficient professional is marked by the parameters of the number of clients he gets and the earnings he has. Thus, professional success is the measure of a professional. Professionalisation leads to cut throat competition and malpratices, evils of which is sometimes very blatant.

---

1. M.D. Bayles, *Professional Ethics*, California, Wardsworth Publishing Company, 1981.

Also notice that professionals are allowed to charge the clients and collect some fees against their service. This method of collection of fees, is somtimes quite complex. Of course, there can be the distinction between professionals hired by the governments and professionals practising with some registration and licence professionals. The question sometimes is that of should the liberal society have welfare programmes and what all the things should it include in its welfare programmes. The concept of basic needs, for instance, keeps changing, if not very frequently. At one time, education, was not part of the welfare programmes. Now it is universally believed that education is one of the basic needs, food, shelter, clothing, medicine being others. Some advanced countries have started including entertainment in the list of basic needs. We need to speak of professionals, not as government agents, but as private practitioners, since modern societies are moving towards privatisation rather than having more and more control over such matters.

Several professionals have felt, perhaps rightly, that they deserve a differential treatment. The laws have to be modified accordingly, the social expectations have to be moulded and appropriate institutions and organisations ought to be built to safeguard the interest of the professionals and the public at large. The positions of professional ethics *vis-a-vis* the general ethics have been the following: (a) professional ethics is nothing but applied ethics; (b) professional ethics should override the norms of general ethics; (c) professional and general ethics are mutually independent and autonomous.

All those who hold the universal ethics tend to think that there cannot be two competing ethics. All situations including the professional ones, the general principles of norms are applicable. Even if there need be of any special considerations, they would be of a different order. As Hare has pleaded, these philosophers tend to say that one ought to make the distinction between meaning and criteria of moral terms. It is possible that in the modern context, we need to sharpen our criteria to use the moral terms less ambiguously and more accurately. For instance, we may have to speak of intellectual properties. The issue may arise whether reverse engineering is stealing or developing a technology. All rationalists tend to claim that reverse engineering is stealing of a sophisticated kind since what one does is to find a way out of the intellectual property issue.

The intention of the reverse engineering is very clear: to unearth the technological know-how of a very profitable technology. Considering the essential service that certain professions render to the society, thinkers like Goldman[2] tend to think that these roles are strongly differentiated. That is to say that the rights of the ordinary individual can be infringed for the same of the larger interest of the society and since professionals serve the larger interest of the society, at least some professions such as police and judiciary ought to have overriding powers as against the rights of the individual. Rights of an individual to move freely within the boundaries of his country is not normally curtailed. However, if there are reasons to doubt the credibility of the individual, enforcement officials may restrict his movement to certain geographical area only from the point of view of the larger interest of the society. This line of thinking leads professionals having upper hand over the individual members of the society. There are yet others, who tend to believe that the general ethics and professional ethics are independent. General norms never change, whereas there is a need to review and revise the professional codes of conduct. No doubt, certain values may figure on both the lists. For instance, one should honour the contracts made is a norm of promise keeping present in both general and several professional codes of ethics. This need not lead one to think that one necessarily leads to another. It is possible to imagine that the same norm is prevalent in two autonomous bodies. For instance, we do find that right to exercise one's franchise is granted by the constitutions of several democratic countries without necessarily losing their autonomy as countries.

Irrespective of the positions that we may like to alien ourselves, we cannot so easily avoid the issue of human dignity in the professional contexts. For instance, some of the professions treat

---

2. A. Goldman, *The Moral Foundations of Professional Ethics*, Rowman & Littlefield Publishers, Inc., 1980, pp. 34ff

their clients necessarily inferior in some important sense. For instance, in general the professionals would hold that what is good for the patient is better known to the doctor than the patient himself; how the treatment of the mental patients have to be carried out is decided by the psychoanalysts; what has to be taught to children at school and how is decided by the experts on education; whether one has the *prima facie* case to file an affidavit is better known to lawyers than their clients; how to manage money and accounts is better known to the financial adviser rather than the owner and so on. From a certain angle, it is alright to say this. But Hare, for instance, would find problems with all these claims since he would feel that individuals have lost their freedom as moral agents. If such important decisions in life have to be taken by others, then one is not enjoying the moral freedom.

It would be a moot point to claim that the decision ultimately lies in the hands of individuals since the professionals act on behalf of their client after taking informed consent. Obtaining informed consent from one's client before acting, is better on the part of a professional rather than act on his own on important matters. However, even informed consent does not make an individual an autonomous moral agent. For instance, it would be odd to say that my doctor has taken the decision to remove a decayed tooth when I myself suggest the doctor to do so. If I know that it is better to remove the decayed tooth rather than retain it; my doctor could not have taken any professional decision on informed consent. If I do not know anything about tooth and tooth decay; then the doctor cannot decide on my behalf how much information do I require to take the decision on the matter. It might happen that I would like to know all the possible consequences before coming to a decision. And added to that if you are an utilitarian, you may have to spend several years calculating all the possible consequences of a single act of removing a decayed tooth before coming to some conclusion. It would not be surprising if the moral agent feels that he has to re-calculate the benefits of an alternative considered earlier since the factors have changed meanwhile; the individual can continue the process of calculation till he takes his last breath. What is very likely is that the professional gives informations selectively to the professional so that he arrives at the decision which the professional considers most rational at that time given certain estimations on the basis of the past professional experiences and knowledge. This is far less than what is desirable if we have to claim that each and every individual is a moral agent and it is the client who takes the decision even if he consults professionals.

II

The second argument that we would like to consider is based on the findings in biology. We are aware that some plants do not have seeds. A new rose plant is produced by planting a stem. The same is true of several creepers. You cut a part of the creeprer and plant it elsewhere. There are one cell organisms which divide themselves and become two. Amoeba and paramecium are good examples of this kind. Similar process is found in higher organisms. Cells multiply and the organism grow. Occasionally, an egg may be accidentally divided after fertilisation resulting into identical twins. In principle, identical twins are clones.

Genetic engineering has succeeded in producing transgenic tomatoes. They have used genes of animals to produce tomatoes which last long. These transgenic tomatoes take twice the time to ripe than the normal one. Transgenic salmon which weigh 40 times more than the normal one are being produced. It seems that transgenic pigs are produced to increase their reproductive capacity. Rat genes have been transferred to pigs in an attempt to increase their reproductive capacity.

If we grant life to plants, we have the difficulty of giving identity to plants, especially to those which do not have seeds. We do not know whether to call the new saplings of old rose plant new plants. Similarly, whether to treat the part of the creeper cut from the old one a new creeper. Similarly, whether to consider identical twins two different individuals or the same individual.

We do treat identical twins two individuals, and we need to consider Dolly the cloned sheep a new animal. We do not have any epistemic problem in identifying these individuals as different. But a metaphysician is faced with the problem of consciousness. Should he say that Dolly has the same self which its donor had? To say that the same self could exist in two bodies has problems for transcendentalists. If they are two individuals, then the question is: is consciousness divisible?

Moreover, we seem to speak of two levels of consciousness within an organism. We spoke of division of cells: we also spoke of Dolly as an individual. Since there are innumerable cells that constituted Dolly, shall we say that Dolly has two levels of consciousness? At one level, Dolly is constituted of several life forms; and at another level, Dolly is only one individual. Which one of them is philosophically sound? Or shall we say that higher order organisms have several layers of life? Should we speak of several selves forming one organism?

Dolly has been cloned from an adult sheep. Dolly has disproved one of the laws of biology. The assumption that once animal cells go through the mysterious process of differentiation, and become a particular type of cell, they cannot go back to being undifferentiated is proven wrong by the Roslin discovery. Dr. Wilmut's work has made a set of cells forget what they are and start all over again as if they were undifferentiated. This has opened up the possibility of producing clones from adult human beings.

Like Cārvākas, we may say that consciousness is nothing but an epiphenomenon. If we embrace this or similar stand, our notion of human being changes drastically. There would not be much difference between transgenic tomatoes, transgenic pigs and human beings. All of them are what they are due to the genes. There is nothing over and above the physical combination of molecules in a living organism. We are forced to say that the resultant consciousness is nothing better than what we notice in a computer. The relationship between a software and hardware may be cited here.

A certain hardware permits certain software to operate. Given a certain hardware, e.g., a Pentium Personal Computer, the first level of organisation could be Disk Operating System, Windows, Unix or Linux. Once there is the operation system, it has the way of responding to what is given exactly the way a conscious being might do to what it perceives through the senses though a simplified version of it. Within an environment, whether it is DOS or Unix or some other system, further softwares can be loaded and made to work. The second level of organisation can be the specific programmes which would respond differently than the operating system itself. For instance, Lotus programme for date storage within DOS responds differently than the DOS itself. Similarly, we can speak of Unix as the operating system and speak of VI as an editor working within the enviornment of Unix. Networking, whether it is Local Area Networking or the Wide Area Networking, can be considered yet another level of organising. The systems interact and they have their own way of responding to the signals from outside.

The reference to computer is only as an analogy and we are interested in knowing whether speaking of organisation in different levels would help. Both biological systems and the computers seem to work at different levels and they seem to ineract in a certain way. If there is some logic of organising horizontally, there is different logic of operation vertically. When it is the matter of vertical relation, we speak of systems and meta-systems. One level of organisation has to relate itself to another level of organisation.

Biologically, when the cancer is detected, it is not the failure of the system at the horizontal level. The cells know how to multiply, produce proteins, but fail to limit the process of multiplication when their number is adequate. And similarly, the patients suffering from AIDS lose their ability to fight the foreign invaders. They lose their meta-level ability of sustenance, and thus, any disease can take over the biological system leading to death.

How does a higher order system work? There seems to be a certain relationship between the two levels. Higher order system cannot exist without the lower order system. That is to say, if there are no life to cells, the higher system cannot exist. For instance, one of the reasons why cancer leads to death of an individual is that the cells of vital organs die because they grow beyond their own size and in number as a consequence the food, oxygen are not adequate. As a consequence, the cells of vital organs die and the result would be the death of the individual. Also note that thc death is inevitable if anyone of the vital organs fail. The brain, the heart, the kidneys and lungs have to be in normal condition to sustain life. If one may like, we may make three levels of organising life. One at the level of cells, another at the level of tissues forming organs having metabolic activities.

Should we say that there could be yet other levels lower than the cells on the one hand and higher than the conscious. Cells having nucleus, chromosomes, cell membrane seem to have been constituted by further lower level of life forms. Cytoplasm is the fluid in the cell containing mitochondria and lysosome. Mitochondria which acts as a respiratory organelle in the cell; lysosome a form of enzyme kills the old cells. Different constituents of the cell come together to synthesise protein exercising surprisingly high order of freedom and choice. These activities are levels lower than the cells themselves. In contrast, we speak of collective consciousness, public opinion, ecosystems, etc., which are essentially higher level of organisation.

It is clear that reductionism is not possible. And hence we need to speak of autonomy at least at two levels. The cells have their life and driven by their life principles and the conscious being has its own volition. And physicalism is necessarily wrong in the sense that higher order process of thinking cannot be reduced to the level of thinking at the lower level.

The question that naturally arises is: what is the relationship between a lower order and a higher order? We spoke of one way order where the presence of the lower order was assumed to be essential for the existence of the higher order. However, the relationship with the lower and the higher could be much more complicated each level having its own autonomy and yet having some irreducible physical dependence on the lower level. Higher level of organisation does not seem to be devoid of any control over lower level. Mental disturbance produces biological disturbance. The strong desire to live makes the lower level orgnisms to act with swift and courageous manner. Anxiety, fear, restlessness, sleeplessness act on our body. Higher level of imbalance leads to chaos at the lower level and so on. This interdependence between the higher and the lower level is much complicated than what we perhaps can estimate.

The metaphysical issue that we face is the following: if higher forms of life cannot exist without the lower forms of life, then highly developed individuals like human beings cannot exist without the lower forms of life. Moreover, the development in genetic engineering opens up the possibility of producing transgenic organisms including human cloning. Thus, the decay of the body results in the death of the being at the higher level and there does not seem to be any possibility of life after death. And similarly, if we have already produced clones, the consciousness may continue to exist in another form.

Since the genetic experiment shows that there is no ground for the metaphysical notion of self, religious or metaphysical form of humanism is not possible. The movements against human cloning can only show our present concern; it cannot answer our metaphysical issue of the consciousness or self. Therefore, our humanism ought to lie in the world governed by the life principles. Therefore, one may argue that life itself has to be respected and admired. Animals, birds and plants cannot be excluded from our moral considerations.

Humanism as Philosophical Anthropology

Manjulika Ghosh

I

THERE is no definitive model of humanism. While some of the major and most influential ideologies of the past have been put into question of safely disregarded humanism stays on as a reasonable name to describe some of our more respectable ideals. However, it means different things to different people and sometimes it is used as a soothing sound signifying next to nothing. Anybody who wants to take it seriously must try to explain the meaning and significance of the particular variety of humanism he finds most acceptable.

Humanism is often looked upon as an heir to the Greek way of thinking. The Protagorean principle 'Man is the measure' documents not only humanist ideal of the Greeks of that age, but also marks a humanist tradition emphasising the human life, human case and human cause. The difficulty of the Protagorean maxim is, it does not tell us what sort of man is it that serves as the measure. Man is capable of greed, hatred and lust; he can also be an 'angel of surplus'. It is not clear, whether it is a Ghenghis-Khan-like-man or a Buddha-like-man that provides the standard. For that matter, Christianity offers a definite ideal of man in the person of Jesus. He is not only the son of man, but also the son of God. As such, Jesus holds out the human possibilities, what man can become.

II

In the context of this paper I would like to consider humanism as lying within the domain of philosophical anthropology. If we try to state the problematic of humanism clearly, we find that every form of humanism proceeds by way of asserting general propositions of definitional nature, and these are offered in answering the question, 'what is man?'.

Max Scheler coined the term 'philosophical anthropology' in order to designating such endeavours. Thus, as I have stated above, the problem of humanism may be appreciated as the problem of philosophical anthropology.

Humanism or philosophical anthropology has its own issues and problems, and these demand philosophical resolution. If we should care to look back to Kant, we shall see that he, in the Doctrine of method part of the *Critique of Pure Reason* raises the question, 'what is man?' and considers it to be the most basic issue to be settled before we address ourselves to answering such questions 'what can I know?', or 'what I ought to do?', etc. It is so since upon the concept of man put forward in answering the question 'what is man?' our responses to the other questions would be of avail. The point is that we come across in Kant, a self-conscious effort in raising and answering the philosophical issue of humanism. It is well-known that Kant's epistemology is humanistic. It is human knowledge that Kant finally settles for in the debate between dogmatism and skepticism, a refusal to remain within the bounds of sense. There is then Kant's insight that human beings have the prerogative of having a 'transcendental character', i.e., freedom is the definiens of man. This alone ensures man's *dignity*, 'the supersensuous substratum' as Kant calls it in the third *Critique*. It should be unexceptionable to say that Kant's attempt in his critical career has been one of restoring and ensuring man to the possibility of being a moral actor, and finally delighting disinterestedly in entertaining representations. In his essay on Enlightenment Kant sets forth that man's search for self-identity consists in gradually freeing himself from various bondages or 'teuteleges', as he calls it, through self-consciousness. If that be so then aspiration for freedom, be it in knowing, in acting, and in feeling, constitutes or rather defines man's humanity. It is this 'humanity' that Kant calls us to respect not only in one's own person but also in others. And this is *humanism*.

III

When we ask the question, 'what is man?' in philosophical anthropology there could be two ways of answering such a question. One is Plato's way, i.e., to spell out the essence of the notion of 'man'. Adoption of this way, i.e., interpretation of human nature as human essence leads to what is called essentialism; which is often looked upon as a fallacy. This may be true in cases, but the other side of the picture is not happy at all. The logical analyst denies that the 'theory' of man is a matter of completed cognition. But in so denying the logical analyst in fact says that the essence of man is unknowable.

The other way is Wittgenstein's way. Acccording to it, instead of asking 'what is man?' one should ask "what is the concept of 'man' like?". We are not to ask for the meaning of the term 'man', we should, we are told, rather ask for the *use* of the term. It follows that within the Wittgensteinean framework, a theory of man becomes logically impossible, for 'man' cannot have a system of necessary and sufficient properties. 'Man' is an open concept. This means that it is impossible to identify some necessary properties of 'man', fixed and immutable, because new human possibilities may appear in history. The conditions of the application of the concept will be changeable too. We need not follow Plato's way, nor do we have to be an agnostic as the logical behaviourist either. Since an espousal of behaviourism would render philosophical humanism descriptive. One could, in Wittgenstein's way, at best, have empirical generalisations to the effect that certain types or kinds of *homo sapiens* are called 'man' in a linguistic group. One might examine them, and one could never arrive at the ultimate significance of being a human being in moral or spiritual sense. Hence, a sort of non-naturalism keeps teasing us. It seems impossible to derive humanism from a descriptive survey of man. This may have, perhaps, been the reason why locutions as *tvat vam asi*, or *aham brahmāsmi*, etc., are never regarded as empirical generalisations. They are unique in being grasped in a different manner, or intuitively apprehended.

IV

To say that, of course, is not to solve the problem. It is better to be honest in confessing our helplessness in getting along with such locutions, and at the same time, not explaining them away with the help of fashionable philosophical terminology. The model assertions of humanism are usually made, we have already observed, in the form of general propositions, it does not matter which humanistic persuasion is at the back of them, whether it is that of Aristotle, or Kant, Tagore or Gandhi. This logical peculiarity bears an appearance of metaphysical locutions, i.e., they are neither validable nor falsifiable. From this fact it does not follow that they are utter non-sense. They are seriously intended, and employed with concern and commitment.

It must not be supposed that the statements of philosophical anthropology are not confirmable. The paradox of confirmation does not beset them as the general statements of humanism are not inductive generalisations. How are then they confirmed?

The assertions of philosophical anthropology are rooted in existential perspective. By 'existential perspective' may be meant the assumptions or ways of viewing existence. The perspectives may be psychological or introspectively discerniable states of consciousness such as the Vedāntic concept of man overlaid with sheaths. It may be political or economic as in Aristotle or Marx. It could be evolutionary and self-exceeding as in Śrī Aurobindo. But what matters is the perspective, and its concilating power in subsuming other perspectives.

V

A comparative study of the varieties of humanism discloses these existential perspectives. These refer to assumptions about the world and human nature, images of man, etc., operative in a theory of humanism. The term 'existential' refers to a way of viewing *existence*. It is to be distinguished from the term 'existentialist', which designates one special theory about existence. An existentialist EP would be one type of EP.

There may be various EPs. But all of them would be characterised by their views of the world, its properties, man's nature and conditions insofar as these enter into the understanding of human processes and judgements. An EP may include a particular view of human nature and his dominant aims, a particular theory of man's faculties, intellectual, emotional, practical (volitional or conative) and their relations and an image of the self.

The EP is a *stage-setting* for humanism. To elaborate the theatrical metaphor, we may think of the scenic *space* of humanism — the issue of what goes on within himself and other individuals, between himself and a group, between himself and the cosmos. The time may be here and now, the past or future or concern with the eternal. The *dramatis personae* may include gods as well as men (as in Kant), or men alone, or whole groups, i.e., nations, classes (Judaism, Islam, Marx). Or, it may be the central figure of the individual man (Sartre). At times the actor may be some part of man (Descartes' *Cogito*), a soul (Vedānta), a rational element (Kant) or even a superego (Freud). Rational elements make a wider class, from Kant's consistency or Bentham's calculations.

VI

It is needless to say that there would be no *the* theory of human nature and, therefore, no *the* humanism. The different theories are not necessarily incompatiable with each other. Unless one has an ideological or personal commitment to a particular theory, one will probably see them as emphasising different aspects of the total truth about man. Each one of the different theories has made a positive contribution to our understanding of ourselves, of others and our place in the universe.

This may, again, take the shape of further query and answer. Some such queries are the question of freedom against determinism, consciousness *vs* matter, the nature of moral values, etc. The description and analysis of these need not involve any transcendent hypothesis about the nature of the universe, whether Platonic forms or supersensible phenomenon, like God. Perhaps, such description and analysis can form the basis of a new vision of humanism, for such is the nature of progress in philosophy.

Is Humanism Sufficient to Explain Religion?

A. Ramamurty

An attempt is made in this paper to show the limitations or inadequacy of humanism as a possible explanation of religion, which also may go against its claim that human reality is its own explanation. Most of us tend to agree with the basic claim of humanism that human reality is self-sufficient and self-explanatory. Religion is traditionally regarded as the ultimate explanation of human reality, especially his higher nature, but according to humanism it is the human reality that tolds the key to understanding religion and can provide a satisfactory explanation of religion. Now the problem is whether understanding of religion is essential to understand human reality or is it the other way round, that is, understanding of human reality is sufficient to understand and explain the nature and meaning of religion. We normally think that nature is sufficient to explain everything except human reality as human reality involves something which is non-natural and therefore non-empirical. On the other hand, if we think that nature is all that is, and scientific or positive knowledge of it reveals everything about it then to bring in religions to understand and explain human reality will be superfluous. While most of us think that the various empirical disciplines which study human reality like psychology, anthropology, etc., are sufficient to understand and explain the reality of man, religion asserts that there is something in the reality of man which cannot be understood and explained by the empirical disciplines which study man without resorting to some kind of reductive analysis.

What is human reality? Much about man can be studied and

explained in terms of the various empirical disciplines. Most of the human feelings, urges and aspirations have only biological or psychological or sociological significance, and are therefore amenable to biological or psychological or sociological analysis and understanding. But is that all about man? What about those human feelings, emotions and aspirations which we normally consider as constituting the higher nature or essence of man? Humanism recognises the higher nature of man. It does not deny the presence in man or certain higher and nobler feelings and aspirations like love, devotion, sense of self-sacrifice, etc. Do they have only a biological or psychological or sociological significance and explanation? It is in respect of the higher nature of man there is a controversy between spiritual traditions and religion on the one side and the empirical disciplines on the other. How to understand and explain the presence in man such higher feelings and aspirations which have no known natural or empirical purpose to serve. Of course, the empirical disciplines and some of the schools of philosophy try to find or explain their value and significance in terms of man's need to adjust himself effectively with the environment, including social environment. I am not interested in discussing the adequacy of such an understanding. Humanism is conscious of this problem but it nevertheless maintains that the higher nature of man is purely human and does not point to a reality which is other than and beyond the reality of man.

Human ability to respond sympathetically and positively to such higher and nobler feelings of love, devotion, sense of self-sacrifice, etc., when seen in others as well as his experience of them, though occasionally, needs satisfactory explanation. They are, no doubt, human though all of us may not be clearly aware of their presence within ourselves, and may not also be able to experience them clearly and intensely as some others do. Nevertheless, they are a fact of human existence, and most of us do not pay serious attention to them as they do not seem to serve any of our ordinary of empirical purposes.

Now humanism asserts that man is the real sources as well as the explanation of his higher nature or his essence. But by a process of abstraction man estranges himself from his own higher nature or essence, and then by projecting or objectifying it he imagines the reality of God as the real source of all that is good and noble in himself which constitute his real or higher nature. As a result of this process man becomes alienated from his own higher nature, and looks to God for appropriating or attaining it. Thus the reality of God supposed to be the ultimate source of all that is good and perfect is a human projection or an objectification of man's higher nature. And by projecting or objectifying his own higher nature in the form of God man alienates himself from his own higher nature and feels himself helpless and accepts his dependence upon God for appropriating all that is good and noble, as well as for their fulfilment. And to the extent man alienates himself from his own higher nature to that extent he not only feels himself dependent upon God but depreciates or despises his own worth and significance. Human dependence upon God for all that is good and perfect result in his identification of himself with his lower nature which is imperfect and sinful in comparison to what is higher and good. By attributing all that is good and perfect, which really belong to him and constitute his higher nature, to God man develops a poor image of himself in terms of his lower nature. And in an effort to appropriate to himself the divine nature or attributes man feels that he has to surrender himself to God or become completely dependent upon Him. And to be completely surrendered to God or to become completely dependent upon Him man has to deny to himself any worth and significance. These two form the two aspects of the same process. More a man denies himself he considers himself more in communion with God or is religious and spiritual, and more a man asserts himself and his individuality and freedom he thinks he is not religious or is alienated from God. Thus perfection and fulfilment of human existence, according to religion, depends on man's total surrender of his individuality and freedom to God.

In this process man loses his autonomy and freedom, and becomes dependent on God or on religion for all that is good and noble in himself, as he feels that he cannot be really good and perfect without being helped by God or without receiving the grace of God. Thus by attributing to God all that is good and noble in himself man becomes morally and spiritually poor as it were, as he identifies himself with his lower nature. And the hope of redemption from his sinful state of existence or from his physical state of existence which man despises will then be placed in the hands of God.

This is the case with almost all the religions as all the religions insist that without giving up or conquering or transcending one's sinful state of existence or the state of ignorance or his ordinary or physical state of existence man cannot hope to be religious or spiritual, and that to a large extent depends upon the help one recieves from without, be it God or Guru. Man's physical state of existence or his lower nature is seen as opposed to his higher nature or his spiritual state of existence, and therefore man thinks that on his own or in terms of his own efforts he cannot overcome one and attain the other. Thus the greatest disservice religion has done to man, according to humanism, is to deny the possibility of human perfection and happiness without depending upon God or without giving up or overcoming his simple human nature or without dying to himself. As human perfection and happines are conceived in divine terms by all the religions, real happiness and pefection are not possible for man without participating in or partaking the divine nature which is not possible without negating or denying his ordinary state of existence. On his own man cannot attain such perfection and happiness, and the ordinary or secular or empirical state of perfection and happiness of man are not real perfection and happiness. And no religion admits the possibility of human perfection and happiness without the active help or intervention of God. But the problem of human perfection and happiness, according to humanism, arises basically because of the process of alienation as a result of which man is estranged from his own higher nature, and seeks the help or grace of God to regain it.

Thus the real source of explanation of God and religion, according to humanism, is man and the process of his alienation from his own higher nature or essence. Therefore, humanism seeks to restore to man, his dignity, autonomy and freedom, which are deprived of him by religion.

Now, we may think that the humanistic explanation of religion is plausible and meaningful, and therefore religion in the traditional sense is redundant in the life of man as it does not really understand the reality of man. Nevertheless, humanism accepts that human perfection and happiness involve society and certain social processes. For instance, the idea of justice is human but to realise it or for its active realisation and fulfilment man has to depend upon society.

It is not sufficient that man has the capacity and will to be good, happy, perfect just, etc., as their realisation and fulfilment involve society or other individuals. Though they are basically human they cannot be achieved or realised without society The feelings, emotions and aspirations of man are human but their realisation and fulfilment involve society as they are not their own fulfilment; and man cannot be happy without their fulfilment. In other words, they point to or are directed towards something outside of man for their fulfilment or as the possible source of their fulfilment. Hunger, fear, love, etc., which are human are directed towards a reality which is not man himself. All the desires and emotions in man find thier fulfilment in a reality which is not man himself but something other than and beyond man. They are directed towards a reality which is other than themselves or man, and no man is happy just by having them or experiencing them. No one is happy without their fulfilment and their fulfilment involves a reality other than man himself. This is true with regard to the lower nature of man.

Now, are we not justified in extending the same logic to the higher nature of man so that a reality other than and beyond man, call it God or the divine, could be the possible source of its fulfilment. And what could satisfy or fulfil an urge or a desire or a feeling is somehow indicated within the nature of them so that what could be the source of their fulfilment must have something in common with them or be similar in nature with them. As pointed out earlier certain of the feelings, emotions and aspirations of man which are not meaningful and even useful in relation to man's empirical life may however find their significance and value in revealing and in pointing to a reality which could be the source and object of their fulfilment. Is it not meaningful to think that the higher nature of man which manifests itself in the form of love, devotion, etc., is an indication or a sign in man about the nature and existence of the divine or God? The various emotions and urges in man find their fulfilment not in themselves but in a reality which is other than man. Hunger has no meaning if it cannot be satisfied by food. Similarly, disinterested love or love in its pure form and pure devotion which cannot find their complete fulfilment in terms of man's empirical or secular life are directed towards a reality which is more than man, society and nature. Ordinary feelings, emotions, desires and aspirations of man are meaningful as they help man in adjusting himself effectively and successfully with the enviornment and fulfilling some of his needs. However, pure love and pure devotion though to some extent are meaningful in terms of their biological and sociological value cannot find their total fulfilment in terms of man's need to adjust himself with society and environment, as man at no time of his existence feels that all his feelings and aspirations are completely satisfied and fulfilled in terms of his empirical life and its happiness. At such moments of his existence man really turns to be religious and seeks a reality that could be the source and object of total and unconditioned fulfilment of himself and his higher nature. That is how the mystics of all religions describe their experience of the divine or God. Mystical experience is a state of total or absolute fulfilment of human existence, especially his higher nature and aspirations, and beyond which one seeks nothing. Such kind of fulfilment and happiness can alone satisfy certain of the human emotions and aspirations, and that is possible only in terms of man's realisation of the divine or God and for which man has the capacity and urge. Thus man's fulfilment and happiness are not possible in terms of himself or in terms of society but in relation to a reality which we call God or the divine, and therefore God or the divine is the real source and justification of religion. Human reality or his higher nature points to the possibility of religion which though has its beginning in man cannot find its consummation or fulfilment in man.

Humanism and Literature

Humanistic Standards in Literary Criticism

Meera Panigrahi

Introduction

THE conception of criticism as commentary and hermeneutic guide needs to be considered when discussing its humanistic imperative. Every object of humanistic study: Chaucer's *Canterbury Tales*, Locke's *Treatise on Human Nature*, even Newton's *Principia* or Darwin's *Origin of the Species*, refers to particular historical and cultural moments. They are generally studied through description and paraphrase. This method is valid for interpretation of texts for readers who find them difficult and unfamiliar. If such interpretation enhances their understanding and shapes their sensibility, the human purpose of criticism is served. If on the other hand, literary criticism is based on certain theories or aims at elucidating theories derived from wide range of disciplines as linguistics, phychoanalysis, philosophy it caters to the taste of a limited class of readers. It even projects the mistaken notion of literature as unsuited to the tastes and needs of a large section of the educated class. A humanist view regards literature as a vast reservoir of traditional and moral values; the accumulated wisdom of society expressed by the best minds in the best way possible. It is of immense value to everyone in society and this is what humanistic literary criticism makes evident by focusing mainly on the human context of literature.

In the post-modern scenario, there is a pervasive influence of what might be called over specialised literary studies dependent on linguistic, psychoanalytic, biological or sociological theories of human behaviour and responses that aim to study man scientifically. They have a way of guiding the writing of contemporary writers. As a result of this trend there is much exaggerated effort to experiment and create new literary forms in order to evoke new ways of looking at the world.

Such a deflection of human concerns in literature and excessive interest in theories derived from 'human sciences' in criticism, together obfuscate reality and distort meaning of seminal texts. The complaint more commonly heard today is that modern criticism's obsession with theory undermines the study of literature in a more fundamental way by questioning its very foundation, such as the idea of the author as origin of a text's meaning, the possibility of objective interpretation, the validity of empirical historical scholarship and the authority of a literary canon. These are traditional humanist principles which modern critical theory is critical about.

Objectives

The objective of this paper is to posit humanistic criticism as an alternative to modernist critical projects. It examines the necessity of a humanistic tradition which makes criticism conceive of its function as the articulation of inherited traditional truths in literature. It proceeds on the idea that the experience of literature cannot finally be analysed by systematised theoretical assumptions, and that literature should not be studied outside the context of the human relations and situations that occasioned it.

Literature and Criticism

The aim of literature is to enlighten and delight. Through aesthetic enjoyment it seeks to diffuse eternal truths of life and help the readers to make sense of the world in which they live. The function of criticism is to carry along from generation to generation the whole freight of the values of culture which Matthew Arnold calls "the best that is known and thought in the world"[1] and to create an

---

1. M. Arnold, "The Function of Criticism at the Present Time", in *Selected Prose*, ed. by P.J. Keating, Penguin, New York, 1970, 134.

ethos which conducive for the production of literary works of a high order. In this respect, the importance of criticism to culture and human development is immense.

One may say that in the twentieth century, the function of criticism is to arrest the dehumanisation of art that has been the result of a scientific-technological view of man and society. It must break away from a practice which subjects all human phenomena to scientific systems of interpretation and must seek an alternative approach.

Humanistic Criticism

Criticism as a humanistic enterprise aspires to the transmission of a fully formed cultural heritage-fully formed truths. It should follow the pedagogic imperative of disseminating what is self-evidently the best that has been thought and said. T.S. Eliot also articulates this view when he argues in "The Function of Criticism" that the end of criticism "roughly speaking appears to be the elucidation of works of art and the correction of taste".[2] Allen Tate in his apology for criticism, "The present Function of Criticism" makes the same point. Tate writes that the function of criticism is "to maintain and to demonstrate the special, unique and complete knowledge which the great forms of literature afford us". He clarifies that by knowledge he means "not historical documentation and information" but the truth of human existence.[3]

In a similar vien Arnold before him defined criticism as 'disinterested' evaluation and felt that an objective critic keeps "aloof from what is called the practical view of things" and resolutely "follows the laws of its own nature, which is to be the free play of the mind on all subjects which it touches".[4]

---

2. T.S. Eliot, "The Function of Criticism", in *Selection Prose*, ed. by P.J. Keating, p. 69.
3. A. Tate, "The Present Function of Criticism", in *Reason in Madness: Critical Essays*, Putnam's, New York ,1941, p. 9.
4. M. Arnold, "The Function of Criticism", in *Selected Prose*, p. 142.

Both Arnold and Eliot indirectly refer to the responsibility of the critic to influence the intellect and emotions of readers and also help in their inner development through the educative value of their writing. Criticism does not merely supplement art. Apart from being a pedagogical hermeneutics criticism is capable of effecting the same kind of vision and critique of the world that literature does. Its aim is not merely to recover the intentional meanings of the artist or as Frank Kermode says to provide "a consensus, a set of foreunderstandings exterior to a text which enable us to follow the text".[5] Criticism can cover wider areas of cultural practice to include questions of politics, semantics, the philosophy of language and social relations along with questions concerning the nature of literary study, its responsibilities and its very objects of study. It can be the source of an all encompassing knowledge and as Arnold had argued in *The Study of Poetry*, it can be a substitute for religion. What remains to be seen is whether the modern mind is willing to accord such high destinies to literature and literary studies or persist in relegating to it a much narrow space as an academic discipline to be studied diligently by a small group of intellectuals in universities.

A humanistic interpretation of life and literature is of immense value not only to the student of literature but also to intellectuals of all disciplines who are seriously trying to imbibe a certain mental resilience to deal with the countless ideas literary and non-literary that the society today is flooded with owing to the rapid expansion of knowledge. Humanism appears to be as much relevant today as at other times because its ideas spring from an organic view of life, a serious attempt to understand and define the human dilemma in a technological society, and a sense of history that is essential to sharpen the perceptual powers of a critic. A reorientation of literary criticism on humanistic lines will act as a sane influence on the tendency of modern critics to generate a plethora of literary theories in a frenzy of experimentation. Humanism contains the power to revitalise the modern dessication and confusion of a mind struggling to grasp such diverse forms of knowledge.

A true humanist is concerned with the seriousness of the

5. M. Arnold, "The Function of Criticism", in *Selected Prose*.

problem confronting the artist in the modern world which is the problem of trying to establish relationships and connections in a fragmented world. Modernism, as Richand Ellman and Charles Fiedelson put it, implies "some sort of historical discontinuity and a liberation from inherited patterns".[6] It simultaneously means deprivation and disinheritance, being set free, and also broken off from the values of a humanistic past. The task of the critic is to recover permanent and universal values. This is a formidable task in a society governed by democratised ideas of politics, art and literature, but not impossible. The critic himself must be well grounded in a stable system of beliefs and values that he must help to propagate and revitalise. In this way he acts as an oppositional and correctional force to the modern tendency for individualism and repudiation of all inherited human values.

Literary knowledge is different from all other forms of knowledge. Literary texts constitute a privileged site where the most important social, psychological, and cultural forces meet and contend. T.S. Eliot also sees literature as a privileged area where humanity reveals its essence. Hence, literary criticism should deal with civilisation, tradition, the mind of man and above all criticism must make apparent "something outside of ourselves which may provisionally be called truth".[7] In this way, then, literary criticism as a humanistic alternative to the study of literature as a 'human science' must be seen ultimately as a subject for pedagogy, the best that is already known and already thought. Hence tradition is central to humanism and culture.

The modernist criticism, despite its attacks on romantic readings of literature, falls short of humanistic standards. For instance, the formalist view instituted by Russian formalism is fallacious because it shows a lack of concern for the meaning and content of literary works. An undue concern with form and technique also succeded in separating literature and life. Concepts like the death of the author, the absence of a unified single meaning of a text, the verbal universe

---

6. Rand F.C. Ellman,. *The Modern Tradition*, Oxford University Press, New York, 1965, p. vi.
7. T.S. Eliot, "The Function of Criticism", in *Selected Prose*, p. 16.

of literature and intertextual correlations further reduced and ultimately negated the world beyond it.

Even existential philosophy which claimed to be humanistic could not bring out the humanist potential to full extent. Jean Paul Sartre's *Nausea* is a clear example of alienation and solecism. The language which was used to depict such fragmentation became distorted, broken and highly personalised, lacking emotive power. Similarly, 'the theatre of the absurd' was an example in drama that reflected the barrenness of modern life. Critical activity in such a field of human emptiness became a struggle to wrest meaning, some kind of literary meaning. It resorted to strategies that legitimised new trends and explored possible avenues to construct, deconstruct and reconstruct theories of literature, thereby to demonstrate the utter futility of revived truths.

Thus criticism which had conceived of literature as a 'slice of life' and a fund of moral instructions for the society, became highly stylistical, obtruse and of no interest to lay readers. There have been many attempts to reinvigorate literature and restore to it its balance and health. Marxist criticism for instance attacks modernist philosophy, its despair and alienation. It sought to fill up the need for belief in something believable other than religion and God. It was primarily a movement against the dehumanisation and atomisation of man inherent in Western industrialism. Marx's philosophy is rooted in the humanist Western philosophical tradition which reaches from Spinoza through French and German enlightenment philosophies of the eighteenth century to Goethe and Hegel. The very essence of his philosophy is concern for man and the realisation of his potentialities. But for many critics now Marxism is inadequate for there is simply too much faith in history, not enough knowledge of man and nature.

In the Marxist view of literary criticism the engaged critic promotes and helps to effect cultural revolution through a political commitment in literary studies. Whether it is political or economic considerations which determine our response to human reality, it is at best a culturally conditioned consciousness that is generated.

Any kind of deterministic theory of literature that subjects human nature to natural, biological, psychological, sociological even the cultural is reductionist and hence non-humanistic. It makes us see human beings as objects, or machines, not a thinking, feeling individual who assimilates elements of his culture but behaves independently on his own right as a human being. Humanism projects the individual as existing in a dialectical relationship with his culture formed by it, as well as participating in its transformation by creative efforts. This he does by making a great tradition of moral values the source of his inspiration.

Although Romantic subjectivity is held in suspicion Humanism acknowledges human subjectivity which modernism rejects but with 'disinterestedness' (Arnold) and objectivity. It believes in an objective truth of humanity that transcends the historical situations in which it arises and therefore also posits a human subjectivity that is transcendental. Above all humanism assumes the transcendental objectivity of humanity which can serve as a vantage ground for the study of literature.

Modern Humanism

Twentieth-century humanism modifies Romantic humanism simply by rejecting individual subjectivity. This rejection took the form of a return to Greek sources of European culture in a 'transpersonal humanism' which went under the name of 'New Humanism'.

Modern humanism like Renaissance humanism consistently takes the form of a new Hellenism. Constant in the disparate texts of modernism and modernist approaches to literature is a return to the Greeks, to a set of classical values which have supported ancient Greek culture from the eighth to the fourth century BC. The values that modern culture needs to retrieve from the greeks constitute what Benhabib describes as four complex presuppositions. These are drawn from the Greek tradition of 'practical philosophy', a practical guide that directs a single person in his or her interaction with the larger culture. For Aristotle, Benhabib argues 'practical philosophy' was a unified teaching of ethics and philosophy in relation to human activity in general.[8]

---

8. S. Benhabib, *Critique, Norm and Utopia: A Study of the Function of Critical Theory*, Columbia University Press, New York, 1986, p. 5.

The first assumption governing practical philosophy is that of a unitary model, a totalised system of what humans do and assume as they go about the business of their lives. It shows humans to be living for a purpose that transcends particular individual and particular cultural moments. In these terms individuals comprise a collective transpersonal 'subject' namely humanity.

Secondly, humanity is the social agent that creates history by its activities and is in turn the real locus and origin of experience for individual humans in history.

Thirdly, human history unfolds the nature and fate of humanity and has its own uniquely human purpose which is to show it both as a product of historical forces and the arbitrator of history.

Lastly the good of humanity lies in the emancipation of the individual who learns to correct the past and the present and to see himself and his new modes of knowledge as one and continuous.

What follows from the above arguments is that man becomes the measure of all things. A belief in a divine order of reality is replaced by a human one, and therefore a society's judicial, political, economical and social laws are to be formed and evaluated keeping moral and not divine sanctions in view. Considering literature and literary studies too, evaluation is to be rooted in purely humanistic ideas, eschewing pure imagination and laws connected with it.

Secondly, a continuous tradition of moral ideas and values become important in the search for perfection. To aim towards perfection is to follow accepted truths and to live up to them. Literature being a repository of ideas of how men live and how they ought to live and be, is a valuable source of such complete knowledge by which individuals perfect themselves and their society. Literature as well as history is of inspirational value.

Thirdly, a bringing together of the political and the ethical creates an unfractured cultural climate whereby the individual and social well-being depend on each other. It puts tremendous moral pressure on the artist and critic to conform to high traditional values that integrate his society and to be vigilant about anti-cultural invasions that degrade human life and culture. Literature of the classic-humanist school posited such a world-view and saw the central character as a hero, who was responsible for renistating the moral order after a period of conflict and duress, Shakespeare's *Hamlet* is a very good example of this. Humanist criticism upheld such participation in political, social, moral proceedings and the struggle within him to remain human despite numerous adversities. Even till the eighteenth century such a world-view was feasible, reason being the medium through which the artist interpreted man and nature and united him with the values of his society.

What was lost in the Romantic culture of the nineteenth century was the separation of political and ethical values which ultimately resulted in the separation between conceptions of self-hood and the community's own well-being.[9]

Transpersonal Humanism

Transpersonal humanism which makes humanity synonymous with objectivity is oppositional to the impersonal formalism of literary criticism. Modernist literary criticism transforms critique into a new dogmatism in its polemical anti-Romanticism. We see the modernist critic engaged in the task of sorting through potential meanings and interpretive options needing practically no human sanctions nor even human existence for its justification.

The humanist Irving Babbitt in *Rousseau and Romanticism* advances a programme for a rigorous interpretation of literature and culture and a total rejection of Romanticism with its erosion of critical discrimination, its "emotional naturalism",[10] and its assertion of individualism independent of culture. The humanism of Babbitt caused him to recast criticism devoid of traces of Romanticism, and have it follow a new direction. His attempt was to reconstitute a neo-classical sensibility based on evident demonstration of ideas from cultural and human sources and sufficient reason.

The New Humanism marked a historical moment of cultural reconstruction. It included the formidable task of establishing a

9. S. Benhabib, *Critique, Norm and Utopia*, p. 1.
10. I. Babbitt, *Rousseau and Romanticism*, Houghten Mifflin, New York, 1919, p. x.

sense of tradition through the substantiation of artistic and critical achievement. At the beginning of the modern era poets like Ezra Pound and T.S. Eliot and critics like T.E. Hulme sought for objectivity in their works. Eliot for instance argues in "Tradition and the Individual Talent" that objective poetry is not the expression of personality. He advocated a theory of impersonality and connected it with his ideas on tradition. According to him each new poem or literary work is an appropriation of previous experience and its expression in a new form or a new combination under the initiation of the individual genius of the poet or literary genius. Eliot thus places 'tradition' as a transcendental idea of objectivity and a frame of reference for literary and moral values available to the individual writer.

Eliot set a tone for modern criticism by asserting that "criticism is as inevitable as breathing and that we should be none the worse for articulating what passes in our minds when we read a book and feel an emotion about it".[11] In this statement Eliot captures the double sense of criticism as an exploration of cultural life and as a way of creating a so-called 'objective' (critical) response to the subjective effects of cultural life. Like Babbitt before him, Eliot conceived of modernism as thoroughly against the Romantic humanism of late Victorian England.

Eliot concludes that a real poet sees beneath the phenomenon of the world and articulates feelings which are not personal. His humanistic expectations encompass not only the presence of a beautiful world for the poet, but the simultaneous presence of beauty and ugliness. A true poetic sensibility is capable of seeing "the beauty and the boredom, the ugliness, the horror and the glory",[12] present in life. To be aware of this dualism requires not the Romantic imagination which idealises man and his self-isolation from an industrial culture, but what Lionel Trilling was to call in

---

11. T.S. Eliot, "Tradition and Individual Talent", in *Selected Prose*, ed. by Frank Kermode, Hartcourt Brace, New York, 1975, p. 37.
12. T.S. Eliot, "The Function of Criticism", p. 106.

1950 as the liberal imagination which takes note of every aspect of reality, leaving nothing out of its purview and trying to reconcile disparate elements of culture. In short it examines culture in all its complexity and variety. It admits the importance and relevance of self-hood which is capable of standing both inside and outside of culture, to observe it critically and to shapen his own self and transform culture by constantly studying his past.

These new humanists call for a complete abandonment of Romanticism's subjective experience and language use and for the development of an emergent modern anti-Romantic critical sensibility. They had faith in human reason to make connections within and among experiences. For them superior art comes out of the knowledge born out of reasoned discriminations and a rational perspective by a subject who links past and present perspectives. T.E. Hulme like Trilling assumes that human beings cannot prosper and grow in a vacuum, that is outside of a cultural medium. He concludes that "it is only by tradition and organisation that anything decent can be got out of people".[13]

Eliot and Hulme were more or less echoing Babbitt; but the most forceful articulation of humanistic standards come from F.R. Leavis. Leavis contends that literature is studied in terms of ethics and aesthetics. He gave credence to literary criticism as an institutional practice and as an approach to culttural criticism. In the Great Tradition, Leavis traces the emergence of Anglo-American novelists involved in an ongoing cultural discourse about values and ethics — instituted mainly by novelists like George Eliot, Henry James, Joseph Conrad and D.H. Lawrence.

Leavis deplored the rapidly increasing multiple determinants of culture that accompanied democratic egalitarianism in education, and he thought they were disastrous for humanity because of their anti-hierachical and socially levelling effects. Leavis felt that it was for the University to save the essential elements of humanism in culture whose moral foundation is in constant peril. The threat comes from the levelling forces of democracy which permits freedom

13. T.E. Hulme, *Speculations*, Kegan Paul, London, 1923, p. 116.

and license in an arbitrary manner. The intellectual elite comprises academicians intent on developing and perfecting culture and its determinants to withstand the influences of any economic, technical or social system.

Leavis conceived of this humanistic revolution as happening through the interventions of the sensible intellectual, the critic whose cultural work advances the good of his or her own community and whose work features "a continuous consciousness and a mature directing sense of values", personal judgements in which values are neither entirely objective or scientific, nor merely private.[14] He calls such a critic an 'organic critic' who must have a 'preoccupation' with "the problem of making the study of literature a discipline — not a discipline of scholarly industry and academic method, but a discipline of intelligence and sensibility".[15] The critic's mind, energetic and resourceful by a long training in the humanities, "will apply itself to the problem of civilisation and eagerly continue to improve its equipment and explore fresh approaches".[16]

A special cultural responsibility falls on the humanist critic in the threatening circumstances of modern culture, the rise of suburban culture as it decentres values. Criticism is capable of creating a cultural frame in relation to which critics can go about the business of probing and understanding the products of culture in a productive way. The appropriate frame for this discussion was first established by Matthew Arnold to orient literary criticism towards its social function. Arnold was Leavis' predecessor in declaring modern civilisation unfit as a vehicle for transmitting culture into the twentieth century. Arnold thought that the first line of defense for rectifying this inadequacy was criticism because of its inherently pedagogic function, its function in showing people how to read.

---

14. F.R. Leavis, *Education and the University: A Sketch for an English School*, Chatto and Windus, London, 1943, p. 15.

15. *Ibid.*, p. 7.

16. *Ibid.*, p. 59.

Conclusion

The task at hand for criticism is to prepare for poetry, by first saving civilisation through safeguarding human values. Once culture has been strengthened and a degree of cultural literacy restored modern culture will then be ready for the reinstituted reign of poetry and art.

The humanistic movement in literature, taken in its totality, calls for the understanding and judgement of culture according to high standards. The aim is to have an enriched cultural environment for literature; especially poetry, a cultural context where good and noble literary works are produced, read and enjoyed for the right reasons by all educated men and women, regardless of class. In a mass society, this is an idea difficult to comprehend and realise. What the majority regard as cultural items is popular art dished out on flat T.V. screens. If we continue to consume such kitsch uncritically, it will difinitely be the death of our self-hood as it will be the end of all art.

The Contributors

Dr. Sarat Chandra Panigrahi is Reader in Philosophy at Utkal University.

Dr. Ashok Vohra is Professor of Philosophy at Delhi University and Former Member-Secretary of the Indian Council of Philosophical Research, New Delhi.

Dr. Bijoy H. Boruah is Professor in the Department of Humanities and Social Sciences, I.I.T., Kanpur.

Dr. Ramesh Chandra Pradhan is Professor of Philosophy at the Central University of Hyderabad.

Dr. Ganesh Prasad Das is Reader in Philosophy at Utkal University.

Dr. Aditya Kumar Mohanty is Reader in Philosophy at Utkal University.

Dr. (Miss) Rajshri K. Jobanputra is a Research Fellow in the Department of Humanities and Social Sciences, I.I.T. Bombay.

Dr. Subhas E. Bhelkey is Reader in Philosophy at the University of Pune.

Dr. Priyadarshi Patnaik is Assistant Professor in English in the Department of Humanities and Social Sciences, I.I.T. Kharagpur.

Dr. Ravi Raj Singh is Professor and the Chairman of the Department of Philosophy at Brock University, Ontario, Canada.

Dr. (Mrs.) Mahasweta Chaudhury is Reader in Philosophy at the Calcutta University.

Sri Vinay Hardikar is Executive Editor, *The New Quest*.

Dr. (Mrs.) Tandra Patnaik is Reader in Philosophy at Utkal University.

Dr. Sharad Deshpande is Reader in Philosophy at Pune University.

Dr. Narayan Chandra Padhi is a former Principal of Government College in Orissa.

Dr. P.R. Bhat is Professor of Philosophy in the Department of Humanities and Social Sciences, I.I.T. Bombay.

Dr. (Mrs.) Manjulika Ghosh is Reader in Philosophy at North Bengal University.

Dr. A. Ramamurty is former Professor of Philosophy at the Central University of Hyderabad.

Dr. (Mrs.) Meera Panigrahi is Reader in English in B.J.B. College, Bhubaneswar.